G000071298

LI[
VISION

FIND YOUR
LIFE'S PURPOSE

First published by O Books, 2007
O Books is an imprint of John Hunt Publishing Ltd.,
The Bothy, Deershot Lodge, Park Lane, Ropley, Hants, SO24 0BE, UK
office1@o-books.net
www.o-books.net

Distribution in:

UK and Europe
Orca Book Services
orders@orcabookservices.co.uk
Tel: 01202 665432 Fax: 01202 666219 Int. code (44)

USA and Canada
NBN
custserv@nbnbooks.com
Tel: 1 800 462 6420 Fax: 1 800 338 4550

Australia and New Zealand
Brumby Books
sales@brumbybooks.com.au
Tel: 61 3 9761 5535 Fax: 61 3 9761 7095

Far East (offices in Singapore, Thailand, Hong Kong, Taiwan)
Pansing Distribution Pte Ltd
kemal@pansing.com
Tel: 65 6319 9939 Fax: 65 6462 5761

South Africa
Alternative Books
altbook@peterhyde.co.za
Tel: 021 447 5300 Fax: 021 447 1430

Text copyright Tracey Ash 2007

Design: Stuart Davies

ISBN: 978-1-84694-056-9

A CIP catalogue record for this book is available from the British Library.

Printed in the US by Maple Vail

LIFE VISION

FIND YOUR LIFE'S PURPOSE

Tracey Ash

BOOKS

Winchester, UK
Washington, USA

CONTENTS

For our daughters, Scarlett Grace and India Mae

" Life Purpose is the most important core, driving force- healing and awakening us to who we truly are. Awakening us to our divinity and destiny. Awakening us into self-mastery and a new world vision of conscious creation and conscious healing. Our connection to the world and universe may finally be understood. "

Tracey Ash, 25 May 2007

ACKNOWLEDGEMENTS

This book has truly been a journey and a gift with everyone I have ever encountered, loved and lost. It is indeed a very special journey for my soul in listening for the truest message of Life Vision. With eternal love and gratitude to my daughters Scarlett and India Mae who have truly inspired my life vision and this book with every step. Martin, for his artistic vision and his intelligent questioning. My family- my mother, father and brother who are also so deeply important in my journey in writing Life Vision. My dear friend Caroline Horn, for her support over many years and her vision of *The Awakening System*. Her professional advice and inspiration. And to Obooks- John Hunt, Kate Rowlandson and Maria Watson.

I am honoured to love and work at The College of Psychic Studies, my 'other' home and inspiration. In particular, Suzanna McInerney (former President) for recognising my potential from the start of my professional career. With special thanks to Max Eames (President), Christine Byron, Joe Bailey, Octavia Kenny and Jeannie Karr. All of you have magically contributed in one way or another in my journey developing my work. My first teacher, Audrey Ringwald, and teachers who have truly inspired me- Gerrie March, Sue Minns, Arthur Molinary, Elizabeth Roberts and Richard Ward-Roden. Especially the finest mediumship of Ivy Northage in my first visits to The College of Psychic Studies- when I watched her work. With special thank you to Richard Dancer and Kay Stirling.

Carolyn Burdett who saw the importance and potential of *The Awakening System* as a column working with life vision.

Violet Hill Studios- Pauline and Tony Gromann and Tofte Labyrinth and Healing Centre - Suzy Castleman for eternal kindness and support of *The Awakening System* Programme. Eleni Fouti- her inspiration taking The *Awakening System* to Corfu.

Finally, to every client who teaches me so much. And for the case studies in this book, I will forever be grateful, for sharing your stories and your journeys into empowered life vision. Anguela , Tony, Caroline, Sue, Maria, Charlie, Johanna, Hawa, Ethan, Carolyn, Jeremy, Malachi, Liz, Lena, Joanne, Tony , Tony and Isobel.

Very special thanks to the reception staff at The College of Psychic Studies.

INTRODUCTION

There is a *life vision* for each of us and the purpose of this book is to help you activate yours. I am a modern Life Visionary and a modern Life Healer. There is no separation between these two roles. I am a soul coach, I am a soul healer. Powerful psychic insight, life vision transformation and life power tools that can change your world. Discovering your life vision is a healing and inspirational process. I can provide transforming techniques to help you awaken your own, individual vision and reveal to you your full potential for living. Through this you can discover your freedom; you can discover new high levels of energy; new levels of insight and inspiration for self and for living in the modern world. You can discover how to heal your life; and you can be more powerful than you could ever imagine in creating your world.

There is an authentic power within us which can be awakened to enable us to live every moment of life with new energy, new inspiration and new insight being activated for modern living and awakening. You can change your energy and reality right now! This book pinpoints why awakening to our life purpose is so important at this time. From 2007 our perspective of empowered life vision is being activated- inspired and inspiring, creative and healing, magically manifesting. It is needed for all of us to share in developing a dynamic global vision, one that will accelerate humanity's evolution and understanding of divinity.

I have been psychic since childhood - it has always been part of my life. It has brought visionary insight that allows me to access life purpose in others; activating empowered life purpose; awakening their life power tools, transforming their deepest wounds and limitations. I can access *life purpose* in minute detail- locating the drive of life purpose in every facet of their life- accessing detailed relationship patterns, career information and key places to move to where it will unfold. Understanding *life purpose as the healing and creative tool* in your life is key. Life purpose informs you of who you are in every facet of your life vision. And it's not just for individuals - organisations and businesses also have a purpose and vision that is theirs to fulfil.

My work with life vision began with channelling *The Awakening System* almost a decade ago. This system defines and activates our empowered and inspired life purpose. It encompasses psychic channelling, embracing a vision of union and healing between body and soul, heart and mind, spirit and earth. It places the emphasis upon understanding soul, activating high levels of energy, insight and creative manifestation of who we are and who we can be. I access the dynamic, authentic vision of who you are and the infinite potential of who you can be.

A modern spirituality is emerging; one that is inclusive and all encompassing in our modern world. We are searching for an individual and global vision that is not necessarily a religion or a school of thought - but one that can be realistically brought into our modern life. We have all witnessed individuals of the New Age who have retreated so much from the modern world that they have lost the perspective and balance to honour their life purpose. Certainly, isolation in spiritual and consciousness development can bring a deep understanding of Self and life purpose. But in the current global awakening we are being asked to step into the world - and *really live, connect and create from an authentic vision of self* in each facet of our lives.

From the start of 2007 there has been a shift in self awakening and a massive shift in consciousness- how it serves at both individual and collective levels. People are recognising that the lives they have known are rapidly being deconstructed as old limitations and fears rise to the surface to be dealt with in everyday life. For some people there is a deep recognition that the reality of their lives is not authentic. Two decades ago we might have perhaps buried our feelings to be dealt with at a future date. Two decades ago life purpose and authentic life vision might have been put on hold. For others it is an exciting and dynamic awakening into purpose and empowered life vision. A knowing that there are new energies and information to work with each day.

2007 takes us into the new shift- where limitations are being deconstructed and the divine or infinite I is being activated. A powerful individual and global awakening and calling to integrate higher dimensions of energy and soul qualities is emerging. This is when your *life power tools* can be activated. Awakening to your life purpose is key. This is the core energy driving and creating your expanding life vision matrix that deeply connects you with facets of self and the world- you into your life- into the modern world. This is the core of empowered life vision- an accelerated, intelligent, creative life vision that is healing. Who am I? Who is my authentic self? How do I create an authentic world vision? How can I consciously create more for humanity and the world? These are key questions for everyone. These are key concepts for everyone- for everyone to activate in their lives. These are also key questions that will lead us to the very nature of how consciousness is awakening and the insight of humanity to heal and create a new world vision.

In the awakening race towards 2012 the very concept of what your divinity is and can be is being activated in every individual. Whether you need a gentle coaxing into empowered awakening or blasted, deconstructed and shaken into recognising exactly what is limiting and just who you are. So who you are and what your purpose is key as we move into conscious healing and conscious creation of each and every individual. As we move into and beyond 2012, higher levels of physical energy will provide a more powerful energy base so that you can achieve more not only for yourself but a new world vision. But remember this is not only increased physical energy but deep self discovery that will reveal a higher authentic self. The key is understanding and consciously activating who you are. Your life purpose becomes the core, creative driving force now you are awakened. You are no longer limited by a life vision that constantly demands you to wake up to who you are! Expanding and powerfully synchronising you and your life vision exactly where and with whom you resonate. This accelerates your life vision right out into the modern world- allowing you to create from the *infinite I* .

You will also access more of the higher levels of self that powerfully allow you to radiate purer levels of consciousness and energy. This will allow you to acknowledge the higher authentic you in all that you create-expanding your individual and world vision so that you can consciously create from your divinity. Higher levels of energy will allow you to activate powerful awareness once anchored into seconds of insight and inspiration in your daily life or meditation. This will translate into longer periods of insight, self and global insight that will allow you to consciously create who you are, your life vision and world vision. It will also allow you to emanate powerfully and positively- thus healing a far wider world vision. As 2012 to 2025 accelerates, you will consciously acknowledge that you will become more by allowing the old to dissolve and move into empowered perspective of self and a higher divine reality that will allow you to heal, create, transform and rapidly manifest your life purpose and life vision. You will have insight and some of you- even access to telepathy and instant creation in your lives.

From 2007 to 2025 human consciousness is transforming, awakening and is being powerfully healed within the destiny of mankind. This takes on an important and higher perspective as we move out of ME, ME, ME. You are fundamentally entering a new individual and world vision where your purpose unfolds and relates with a world vision dynamic. Dissolving the I. It is an exciting time when as we reach into who we are; we are reaching into understanding so much more of the dynamics of the world and the universe and how the unlimited potential of our consciousness can create a reality beyond what we could ever have conceived in the past. This takes us into individual and global alchemy and manifestation. The magic that once belonged to the past within esoteric minds is being awakened once again to play a key role in our awakening- our awakening to our divinity and understanding the role life purpose plays in all facets of our modern world vision. You become the visionary, the creator, the alchemist and the healer.

This is NOT an esoteric vision but a vision that will blend the modern world with powerful awakening of insight, transformation and creativity in living our destiny. It is at this level of consciousness that you can really change your world- consciously creating, inspiring and healing. Your spirituality vision comes to merge in the every day- modern spirituality- correction- not sidelined to new age centres but the recognition that healing is everything and once consciously activated- everyday and every minute available to you and everyone! What you are activating here- is the divine self- expansive- more powerful, more dynamic and infinitely more magical- with the power to quickly manifest a reality that understands and honours your life purpose and global vision. You have a life purpose to live, a unique role to play in the new world vision- awaken. It is such an important time to be awake. Hence- what we have been all calling for centuries- empowerment, flow, energy, insight and creative life vision. So not a life coach, not a mystic- but a modern alchemist gradually changing your perspective and potential for discovering your life purpose and the energy and healing that can be activated once you lock into your divine life purpose. Awaken to this divine knowledge residing *only within you*- that is your life purpose. This is the key to you understanding the power of the *infinite you* and your infinite potential to create an empowered life vision.

Not wishing for a very different life that perhaps even the most dynamic life coach could ever achieve- but very practically addressing who you are- your unique life purpose and life vision- that is truly perfect as the driving force to awaken who you are. Your life purpose is perfect- once you see it as that. It defines and informs you of exactly who you are in every facet of your life. It requires activating- you might dare to awaken, healing and transforming a limited self. You might dare to have a very empowered perspective of you- this is vast- this is where the *infinite I* potential lies to be creatively worked with- you might dare to be who you are. In doing that- you might dare to live your life purpose. You can become the visionary, the healer, the creator and alchemist of your life. The Awakening System awakens you- to just who you are- activating your life purpose- your empowered life purpose and perspective. The Awakening System powerfully activates *infinite I-* this empowers your life vision and awakens the life power tools within you create your perfect life and world vision.

In the current world vision and modern stress it can seem a precariously unbalanced world- at times in meltdown. As we shift into awakening to the very nature and impact of our consciousness upon modern reality, people are beginning to question the reality we have all created. Individuals are asking if they can have a more significant impact on the world around them- perhaps work not as job but as powerful purpose and vision of far greater significance both to the individual and the world. I see this in clients who are stepping into Mind Body Spirit (MBS) for the first time. People with conventional modern careers - as well as those already involved in the MBS field. These are people from all walks of life and from all around the world. They work in business, finance, education, the arts and they include psychologists, scientists, doctors, counsellors, teachers, journalists, parents and children - the list is endless. My clients are searching for insight into purpose and how they can contribute to their own and humanity's evolution. It is my hope that this book will help you, too, on your search.

I can only talk to you through the pages of this book, rather than face to face as my client. I don't know your particular circumstances. That's why, with their permission, I am giving a few of my clients' inspiring life stories. Each story is a true gift. Each unique in the way each individual strives to discover freedom and healing. They will touch your heart and, I sincerely trust, offer hope for the fulfilment of your dreams for self and the world. What they all demonstrate is that we can become who we truly are. Each story defines, in its own way, the most important human quality – love- learning it both for self and the world. If we can discover this for self and others, then we can consciously heal and create the world. This is the most inspiring and healing journey of all- that will lock you into a divine and empowered life and world vision.

The stories are written in the form of case studies and include recorded extracts from one to one sessions. These extracts key into how I work with my clients to inspire powerful transformation . Each case study is accompanied by a programme of techniques from The Awakening System. They will provide a guide so that you, too, can transform your life and change your world each and every day!

Read their stories and follow the techniques. Your perspective on life can be transformed so that living and healing can be powerful and a pure joy. You can embrace life and *fall in love with living!* I trust that this book will enable you to:

Awaken your Life Purpose

Awaken the visionary, the creator, the alchemist and healer

Awaken the *infinite I*

Awaken World Vision

Tracey Ash 2006

CHAPTER 1

THE AWAKENING SYSTEM

There is a current buzz and excitement not only in Mind Body Spirit but also in the modern world concerning *life vision*. People are finding an urgency to discover and activate their life vision in the most vibrant, inspirational and healing ways so that they can live their lives dynamically with a sense of who they truly are in the modern world.

Whether you have been meditating, healing or working psychically for years or are stepping into the world of MBS for the first time, the questions are the same:

- How do I access and live my *life purpose?*

- How do I expand life purpose and live it everyday?

- How can I live my life vibrantly?

- Who and what do I need to connect with to inspire and powerfully activate my life purpose and global vision?

- Where do I need to be?

- What *life power tools* do I need for an empowered life vision?

- What do I need to heal and transform?

We are living in a time of action. By finding our life vision and the power it brings, we can live in freedom and in the knowledge that we can make empowered changes to self and the world. We are experiencing a huge emphasis on individual and world creativity and responsibility. We are being given the opportunity to work from the divine power of our souls-the authentic self. We are being challenged to infuse our lives and work from higher levels of truth and energy in order to awaken us to the immense global and humanitarian awakening that is taking place. We are learning that we can create and achieve more than we ever dreamed. The new awakening is a positive and dynamic era in potential vision and conscious creation of a new self and new world vision.

This positive and dynamic shift in our power takes us into recognizing as individuals- we can work towards powerful change and healing. Whether we are transforming the *limited I* or discovering the new freedom of working from the *infinite I*- it is indeed an exciting time that inspires and transforms a new self and world vision. As individuals we are opening to our capacity to achieve more. This accelerates our world vision to achieve more also. In physical power awakening we are accelerating our ability to be more organised and achieve more than ever before. We are waking to our capacity to truly contribute to self and to the world. This is the new reality. A modern spirituality is emerging - we are searching for an individual and global vision that can be practically and dynamically achieved in modern life.

Modern spirituality incorporates the following:

* Expanding from the *infinite I*

* Empowered life purpose and life vision

* Empowered sensitivity

* Living from an empowered energy base

* Conscious creation of self and new world vision

The Awakening System works with expanding the *infinite I*- the potential of just what your reality can be. It helps you to define and create your life purpose and life vision, combined with dynamic vision and creation of self, that you require to live your life purpose. In *The Awakening System* the emphasis is upon anchoring and exploring the *infinite I* in a fully conscious state so that you can download essential energy, healing and information for self and new world vision. Energy and information that will importantly inform you of just who you are and your potential.

So what do you do if you don't have the time to reflect? What if you are at the stage of knowing but don't know how to access the energy to achieve a more dynamic and powerful life vision? What if you find it incredibly difficult to achieve balance whilst being bombarded by the emerging new realities?

For example: you might find it difficult to sleep whilst waking excitedly to new ideas, new directions, new realities and possibilities for you. You might be discovering just how difficult it is to let go of the *limited I* and step into the freedom that will allow you to create your life vision. You might not know how to shift patterns that have become rigidly stuck.

The question arises: is there more to me than I am really experiencing? How can I experience more?

Many are beginning to discover an authentic power that lies deep inside. In accessing life purpose- the core energy that drives the discovery of who we truly are- we recognise reality resides deep within. When we reach deep into ourselves we begin to recognise who we are and take responsibility on every level. We begin to recognise that every detail in our life is created.- is created by our perception of reality. We begin to recognise that in expanding from the *infinite I* that we can change our world. We equally recognise the limitations of the *limited I* and the way we can create this in our lives. The phenomenal growth in self-help books, new discoveries of cutting-edge scientists and everyday personal life stories confirm this. Yet it is even more than this- because the *infinite I* activates magical creation and healing of life and new world vision.

That is why my work as a life visionary is rapidly evolving with clients in conventional, modern careers- for clients who would have never had considered Mind Body Spirit before. There appears an urgent need to discover and access more within self and the world. Let's take, for example, men and women in career burnout - waking to the fact that there is much more than tirelessly working a sixty hour week leaving no time for much else. Equally, those in business who are vibrantly living their life vision can take their role into helping others whether it is through positive people dynamics within the workplace or vision in business that encourages integrity-based world development. Equally those in Mind Body Spirit who want to expand their work into the modern world. People who have explored deeply on a personal growth level-analysing the *limited I* to frustration- almost leaving an empty shell and the question- how do I access and expand my authentic self? How do I radiate who I am? How do I inspire and expand who I am? This is interesting as there is a balancing of individual qualities- for example- the over sensitive healer activates the life power tools to step into the empowered healer and work in a corporate environment. The exhausted city lawyer no longer copes from the *limited I* and is screaming for an authentic vision of self- the *infinite I*- where vision, healing and creativity is always abundant. So worlds merge!

Psychologists and counsellors experiencing the energy and the feelings of their clients want to discover more in terms of how energy works. They want to know how to access and radiate purer, positive energy levels within themselves that can assist the healing process for their clients. Doctors, too, who are waking to knowing information about their patients are waking to significant increases in intuition.

Individuals are acknowledging that their power is within. Teachers and parents who are searching for new ways to work with children are exploring spirituality concepts, meditation and relaxation. Equally, a housewife waking to twenty years of living her husband's life is searching to discover just who she is. There is an individual and global awakening

- an urgency to access self. In a visibly unbalanced world, with its attendant stresses, people are beginning to question self and the authenticity of life vision and its significant impact on the world around them.

Whatever you need to discover or let go of to activate your freedom will surface. Your relationships might be in meltdown so that you can recognise your authentic power. You might have 'locked in' your spirituality for years – fearing how you can live it in the modern world -but your awakening will direct you how to live your spirituality right 'out there'.

My professional work with life vision began with spontaneously channelling The Awakening System almost a decade ago whilst teaching a class at The College of Psychic Studies, London. This brought a dynamic system that could be applied uniquely to each individual to access, activate and transform their life vision. It enables life-changing insight into self and the world. As I've been psychic since childhood, I have always been able to access life vision. It has always been part of my life yet this experience was entirely different. I was being given a very practical yet highly spiritual system that could be applied to everyone. I have worked with the system for the last ten years with incredible results for those who have participated in it- in awakening soul and the power of life purpose.

The Awakening System defines your life purpose - awakening and activating high levels of energy, insight, creativity and action. It is rather like a multi-dimensional matrix that can be precisely explored and locked into every level and life area. With each level precisely reinforcing and informing your life purpose you can begin to realise how powerful your life and world vision can become.

Your understanding and recognition of self becomes conscious. You are in power and you have the freedom to create.

The system works with four archangels Uriel, Gabriel, Michael and Raphael. At first, I was shocked that I was channelling archangel information. But something new was being directed - without New Age or religious connotations. The archangels are banks of infinite energy and consciousness that can be accessed to help in transforming all aspects of our lives. I discovered that The Awakening System is a tool for powerful self-discovery and transformation. It gives an individual or an organisation access to their precise life purpose as well as accelerating their life vision. As far as I'm aware, this channelled system has never before been published. It is an intelligent and powerfully energising system that inspires us to understand who we are and what is our life vision. It inspires us to live and create from the *infinite I*- from our soul.

It fully embraces modern living and our place within the modern world. It also allows us to access the psychological empowerment and alchemy of archangels that can truly awaken us to who we are. This is important. Throughout the world, people are acknowledging that we are in need of recognising and awakening authentic self; of healing and transforming self and the world we live in. Archangels powerfully activate within us the life power tools to accomplish this through our life purpose. Life vision becomes a reality of who you truly are! There is no illusion.

The Awakening System embraces inspiration and healing. It embraces a vision of union between body and soul, heart and mind, spirit, world and universe. It places emphasis upon understanding who we are and awakens us through a massive shift of consciousness and energy. Activating life vision is just like being able to fully download the energy and intelligence of who you are, easily and vibrantly, from every level.

When we powerfully awaken life purpose- powerful life transformations occur. This brings an encouraging and dynamic challenge for us to create life vision in a brilliant shift of consciousness that will lead us into new and accelerated vision and healing for self and the modern world.

So many of my clients are experiencing accelerated spiritual and personal growth and energy expansion; people who would never regard themselves as spiritual, psychic or healers. It truly is a time of awakening. Helping people who do not necessarily wish to become psychics or healers in the traditional sense, but who wish to infuse their lives with high levels of energy and expansion, that radiate and connect them with the modern world. A healing and creative new world vision- that's really what The Awakening System is exploring.

CHAPTER 2

HOW THE AWAKENING SYSTEM CAN HELP YOU

It is 2006, London, I am immediately engaged by the flow of people in the street - an individual walking along in his own world, thinking; others stopping and choosing to interact. The exchanges of individuals or groups of individuals as they create their day. This flow of people, the momentum and the interactions, can reflect the stop-start flow of your life. At certain times, you can be right there, in the moment and totally connected to really knowing the direction of your life. You feel alive, vibrant, inspired, powerful and dynamic. At other times you might feel distracted, overwhelmed, disconnected or out of control.

As I look closely into the street. I am fascinated with the people. Not only can you be in a city where you can feel anonymous, you can also feel part of a village where everyone knows each other. It is South Kensington. Even amongst all the tourists thronging to the various museums located here, there is a sense of belonging; a sense of place for the people who live and work in this community. This is why, as I watch, I am able to magnify life beyond the individual - beyond visiting tourists. It is as if we can be transported anywhere in the world in our lives where we feel a deep sense of connection to a place and to people. It might be a quiet village. It might be New York or India. When we begin to question just where we belong we begin to trust our hearts.

Watching the 'stop-start' flow of life in the street, I am drawn to how different we all are - the rhythms and uniqueness of each individual. The communication and confidence we use in our daily lives. It is here in South Kensington, a village within a city, that I watch.

I can explore the interactions of people who already know each other. I can take a giant magnifying glass to life; take a slice of modern life and examine it. I could choose not to be conscious of what is happening but, instead, I am energised and vibrant. I am alive and in the moment. It is the creativity of life that captures my attention. I am aware of who I am. I am aware of other people.

Why does one person behave and respond in life in particular ways? Why does one person sit back when another is alive and fully animated? A person walks down the street never looking up whilst listening to his friends. Friends gossiping. Friends talking. Lovers who are so close there is no-one but the two of them. The mother lovingly greeting her children at the school gates. The mother's face in delight when her little ones approach her. The family alive and excited. The business meeting at the café - the career girl animated, focused and ambitious; alive in the journey of career. One friend listening attentively to her friend - the other friend not listening at all!

The girl dreaming of another time and place. The husband and wife barely attentive. Forgetting their history. Some commuters' lives are infused with the stress of modern living. The excited child who has just bought a toy from the toy shop smiles. The building contractors getting the job done. Practical and methodical. Working hard.

As I watch the people, the momentum, the interactions and the 'stop-start' flow, it mirrors the way we consciously or unconsciously choose to create our lives. In the modern world it can at times be all too easy to lose sight of direction. At times, there can be uncertainty between who we are and how we are perceived to be - a gulf between who we truly are and our sense of knowing what is right for us. There can be a great sense of time, energies and demands closing in on us; the demands of modern life. We may draw distractions in an attempt to iron over who we really are. We may also be awakening to a longing to discover and activate authentic feelings. We may feel an urgency to discover our true self in all that we do and in the way we relate to people with whom we connect.

Sometimes we connect with what is perfection for us and easily attract people and situations with which we truly resonate. This is when we are in our true power of our life vision. What if we could learn to attract more of what is empowering for us? Sometimes, we attract too many people and activities and this does not honour who we really are. At other times, we isolate ourselves by drawing upon too few people and activities to support our lives. In terms of modern spirituality it is absolutely key to achieve a life in balance and to do this we need to recognise what is totally right for our own individual self.

Understanding and using our power and light consciously is what we can all now access.

What energises you? What gives you infinite ideas? What gives you infinite inspiration? Infinite focus? Self and world vision? What might you let go in your life? It is more than being in the moment.

It is more than recognising who we are. It is more than recognising multi-dimensional reality. It's about looking into the world and reaching deep into self to discover and uncover who we are. It's about moving beyond being conscious or limited by our healing issues and limitations. It's about moving beyond dreams and inspirations and begin to really transform and connect with what truly energises and transforms who we are.

The key is working with self, the world, humanity and from our souls. There are many reasons why clients come to me for a life vision session and here are some examples of the issues they wish to explore:

- **What is my life purpose?**

- **Why do I have difficulty expanding *who I* am into modern life?**

- **I am dynamic in my career but I have little energy for relationships.**

- **I don't know what to do since Nanny died - we were inseparable.**

- **My work is fabulous yet I feel restricted by it – it is so stressful.**

- **I am unhappy in my relationship.**

- **I am in the wrong job, the wrong place, the wrong everything.**

- **I don't know where to base myself.**

- **What is my purpose?**

The following are synopses of how The Awakening System helped some of my case studies. Their own stories and what I channelled to help them in their sessions are given in more detail in Chapters 5 – 19.

Hawa, 28, felt she had achieved her dream of being a singer but her underlying fear needed to be tackled so that she could live and create more fully. Just what was really holding her back? Incredible fear and the deepest emotional issues that she had buried for decades. As Hawa locked into her life vision she began to see her life unfolding - her healing journey unfolding - so that she could discover love in a partnership and work with children in performing arts. Hawa continues to activate her life vision as a powerful performer.

Lena - For Lena, years of deep spiritual discovery had dis-connected her from the vibrancy and spontaneity of life. Now she activates her life vision with a deep and integrity-based spirituality and every day sees more clearly her potential as a talented performer. The Life Vision programme transformed her spirituality into vibrant living and acceptance of her deep spirituality having a place within the modern world.

Joanne had spent many years deeply healing herself through counselling and deep spiritual discovery and healing. This had led her to travel the world and work with children. The Awakening System programme connected her with a powerful and intelligent sensitivity that could be used to work with people. She transformed her sensitivity by training psychically to create a life power tool. Today Joanne recognises her role as a communicator working with healing and intuitive psychology.

Charlie faced stress and the bereavement of his father in what would have been a career for life, as a stockbroker. This catapulted him into serious illness and accessing just who he was. At 35, his illness was diagnosed as incurable but undeterred he began a journey of self-discovery, working with The Awakening System to provide healing and the courage to overcome illness. Charlie, has now moved into a Master's training programme in psychotherapy.

This is the Awakening. The emergence of authentic life and global vision. We are in a renaissance where our place in the world may be achieved in pioneering, dynamic ways. The Awakening is shaping greater global and humanitarian vision and responsibility. At this time, we can access an incredible mass of information to begin to change the world with responsibility and creativity. This includes high levels of information and consciousness that we have not seen before at everyday levels. The internet is forcing change and pace of learning where, at a click, immense databanks of information are at our finger tips. It is also responsible for rapid awakening global vision and a 21st century renaissance.

Monumental global events shaped this wave of global awakening - 9/11, Africa, Aids, Tsnuami, America and the Middle East, G8, New Orleans, economics, human rights and disease as examples. Startling wake-up calls for humanity to consider and re-consider self and greater global vision and harmony.

More of us clearly recognise what we do and do not resonate with.

Tony, in his 20s, faced AIDS and related complications. He was forced to recognise his power and lock into his life vision to really transform his quality of life. Tony moved swiftly, activating his life vision as a powerful healer - who could indeed heal. He is a fascinating case study who reflects this time of conscious awakening. He found a deep sense of power within to transform, to heal and create. Tony consciously knew his life vision was not working but by working with the Life Vision programme he transformed his perception of just what he could achieve.

Power, insight and knowing are rapidly emerging. Being aware of your truths can sometimes be difficult at first. It can powerfully support or eradicate what you have already in place - work, relationships, health, home, money or creativity.

Caroline was a very bored journalist, with extremely boring work contracts. Caroline's awakening caused her to assess everything in her life- from why she had no love relationship to why she was surrounded by unsupportive friendships. She addressed discovering herself and what she really wanted to do. Life vision sessions helped her to shape a career that would energise and excite her. Children's literature loomed large. The boring journalism fell away and Caroline began focussing on children's literature and the developing of a pioneering education website for schools, libraries, parents and children. Caroline has learnt to live her dreams and realise her potential as a business woman. She is now in a loving relationship.

This is the magical awakening of the *infinite I*. This empowerment and insight can overhaul outdated values, truths and pain. It will positively develop who we are- expanding life purpose and life vision beyond your dreams. It will powerfully awaken you to your role in creating self and new world vision. It brings deepest authenticity, love and respect for self and the world. It helps us to really consider how we can make a difference and how we can really change our world. This is very important as we move into taking responsibility for the way that we shape our world and reality. This is a magical time when conventional and unconventional meet, where the ancient esoteric meets science and technology, where psychology meets spirituality, where business meets modern spirituality and where education is led by the child within. Humanity is screaming authenticity and divinity.

With what and with whom we resonate is primary and highlights our increasing awareness, not only of our own life but of the world's at the same time. More of us are searching with a deep recognition that we must connect within. This power and insight helps us to shape our potential to create, communicate and connect with others, to work together towards dynamic world vision. This can be in our home, community or a larger global vision.

Sue was so deeply sad, when she came for a life vision session. Her grandmother had recently died. Her daughters had grown up though they were still very much part of her life and constantly sought her advice. With a successful interior design career behind her, Sue felt a necessary urge to focus on just who she was. She had spent a lifetime being there for everyone else and felt it was now her time. Now, Sue is alive and focussed upon her life vision. She trained as a midwife and loves just what she can bring to the families she works with. She is fascinated in the bond between mother and child and what she can do as a midwife to really teach parenting skills. This work is now taking her into supportive midwifery that works with the family as a whole.

It is an exciting journey towards vision and balance. People are moving naturally and quickly towards others with whom they resonate and who can co-create with them. More than ever before, there is self and world vision - a dynamic potential between people. Rapid creativity, inspiration, learning and manifestation that goes beyond what has been experienced before. People are recognising higher levels of awareness and inspiration that can't be ignored! And are fast discovering the ability to create more quickly in their lives.

Tony is a global water expert who for many years worked in the public sector. Unfulfilled, he left his work and began searching to discover self. This he did for many years in meditation but he couldn't translate this into his life. The Awakening System allowed him to accelerate his life vision in a very practical way. Tony began writing a book on water to raise public awareness on the world and environment and now travels the world as a consultant.

The challenge of really being who we are is so evident. Now is the time to really face living and being and becoming more conscious of who we are, and what is right and what is wrong for self and the world.

A new code of truths is awakening hearts and minds so that we can understand how we can positively change our world. In opening our hearts and minds to these truths, we can know who we are and the life vision we potentially can create, both as individuals and as groups, to unfold an ever more powerful life and world vision.

Anguela, now in her early 30s, with degrees in business and the arts. In her late 20s, she began to really discover just what a dis-empowered healer she was! She spent so much time giving her power away to everyone she met that there was little energy left over for her. Anguela worked in awakening her life vision to harness her life purpose as a powerful healer.

Johanna came for life vision sessions and to work with The Awakening System Programme over many years. Incredible spiritual and psychic awareness had taken her energy inwards to the point that every life area was over-analysed and without potential. The Life Vision programme awakened Johanna to her incredible gift as a psychology and anthropology student. As soon as study began, Johanna came to life. She is an adult indigo (explained more fully in later chapters) who had lost all sense of purpose and meaning of her life.

A uniquely individual approach to empowering self is emerging. One that encompasses wisdom; making life choices based on our own truths; accessing infinite energy and creativity for living. We are quickly knowing our potential, power and wisdom. Is this really happening? Yes! We are being challenged to find a greater capacity to express self. Our need for balance between the body, heart, mind and soul is essential.

Physical and psychological symptoms of imbalance are fast-emerging, as we are shaken into honouring our divinity and what that means.

Carolyn had low self-esteem and had had a painful lifetime of bereavement. The Life Vision programme transformed her perception of self and her power to be free. She entered into self-discovery and healing. Carolyn is now a dynamic mother, partner and is looking forward to teaching in primary schools.

Personal alarm signals that we are not in powerful life vision can manifest as stress, allergies, depression, anxiety, fear, disease, lack of motivation and overwork; all manifestations of rejecting modern life, life vision and life purpose. Now is the time for creating the peace within and active awareness to connect precisely to expand who we are and life purpose.

It's about connecting and understanding the true nature of authentic self. By stepping into the divine power of the *infinite I-* we can really know and understand this, then we transform and create our world.

CHAPTER 3

THE LIFE VISION PROGRAMME

What is Life Vision?

What is Life Purpose?

Life Vision is the multi-dimension matrix that explores every facet of self. Each facet of self and life- awakening, healing, inspiring you to truly be who you are. Every facet connecting you with world and universe.

Your life purpose- the core, driving force, creation force, healing force- that awakens you to who you truly are. It powerfully awakens you to the infinite I- the authentic self- soul- spontaneously awakening essential life power tools for living. This activates an empowered and expanding vision of self into the world.

Life purpose is the most important healing and awakening tool available to you. Life purpose is powerfully activated through many facets of self, world and universe. It is designed to awaken you. Your life vision is unique. Your life purpose is unique. Through empowered life purpose- your life vision can infinitely inform and expand who you truly are in the world. You begin living not from the *limited I* but the *infinite I*. Once you discover this divine power within- you will expand into the modern world fully awakened in your life purpose. Awakened and inspired by what you can achieve. Awakened and inspired by others and a new world vision of conscious creation and conscious healing.

Purpose and Focus

Let's think of a rather taught needle and thread - dynamically being sewn into the fabric of the world. The way each stitch can make progress and contact with each life area to build and intensify it. The way each unfocussed stitch may weaken the intensity. The way each focussed stitch can create perfection and potential perfection of our life vision. Like the needle and thread, the more conscious we become of our purpose and focus, the more we create a life matrix that powerfully reflects who we are. This is the potential of our life vision.

The needle takes on purpose and precision. Not in the way that the mind can restrict life vision. Life vision becomes a powerful creative tool with you conscious of your role in its creation. Awakened, you can create life in a flow of knowing who you are. You can create life, mindful that your awareness is key and is a powerful creation tool. As you awaken to your life vision, you may become aware that this needle and thread requires greater focus, greater precision. What you experience in self and the world intensifies and awakens who you are and magnifies your purpose and life vision.

Each stitch informs our creative vision and inspiration for living. Each moment can be filled with inspiration and vibrancy. Each stitch has meaning - and even more meaning - as we begin to trust our expertise as visionary, creator, alchemist and healer in our lives.

Like the most powerful visionary, we begin to trust the power of vision- of the authentic self we understand and can create. It is so important - this implicit trust in our own divine power. Not for one second doubting our ability to hold our life vision and to create it. This is expansion from the *infinite I* not the *limited I*. It's rather like an incredible matrix powered by our life purpose and new world vision. A matrix that locks us into the laws and energy of the universe, the world and humanity. The energy and information contained within our life vision and life purpose crucially impacts upon our world vision and vice versa. Going back to the taut needle and thread, imagine absolute precision timing and perfection in each life situation - always, one of choice -indicating that the power is always with us. The choice of where we place each stitch, the choice of which life area. The choice of our focus. It is also really important to consider what requires our attention. What healing issues do we need to let go or work through?

The Awakening System strives for this freedom by activating empowered life purpose and life vision. The life power tools are awakened so that you can dynamically live your life purpose from the *infinite I*. This activates powerful emotional alchemy and empowerment that can transform your perspective of self and your reality. This powers you forward, transforming fear and leaving outdated limitations behind. Your life vision becomes a powerful creative process – transforming, creating and expanding who you truly are.

This is certainly not about dreaming. We are being challenged to really know who we are and inspire ourselves to live our life vision. If we expand from the *infinite I*- we have the divine power to infinitely understand, create and heal everyday.

What is required of you?

An awakening and deepening of who you are and your life purpose. Your understanding of your life vision is key. To awaken beyond the limitations and parameters you have set yourself up to now and to recognise that you acknowledge an *infinite I* and a *life vision* that expands beyond all you have conceived before. Recognise that you can be who you truly are and radiate into the modern world as you have never done before.

Awaken Your Soul And Life Vision Into The Modern World

New world vision includes high physical energy levels, new extended insight levels of awareness, intuition, telepathy and creative vision- that become every day reality. This new level of awareness also allows us to be fully anchored in the modern world. We move into empowered sensitivity. We expand into the *infinite I*. We can consciously create from this awareness. This allows us to firmly create who we are. It awakens a new vision for self and the world- where awareness is key- when we move from creating from the *limited I*- into vision and healing for a new world.

You also recognize how much the modern world supports and informs your life vision. A new world vision awakens your awareness to where creative transformation and healing is required. The awareness flows into vision and conscious solutions. The new world vision is encouraging us beyond- I can't, I won't, its not possible. High consciousness is being fully merged within the physical and material world. The illusion that your spirituality resides in other dimensions or in a meditation is removed. Or that your authentic self is locked inside- a tiny fragment piece of you. You awaken to really connect with all that resonates with who you are and your life vision. This is important as your life vision takes on an expanding perspective - that of global and universal vision - the landscape that you live in; the work you do; the relationships you create. Authenticity becomes key. You become more powerful and more empowered to change your world. You resonate truly with what empowers your life vision – with every facet.

We are being awakened to:

• **Create And Radiate Who We Are In The Modern World**

What you can awaken everyday:

• **Expand Into Infinite I**

• **The Power Of Life Vision and New World Vision**

• **Dynamic Connections To The World**

• **A Powerful Energy Base And Creativity For Life And World Vision**

• **Empowered Sensitivity/Emotional Intelligence**

The activating and anchoring energy of where we live and work is vital. It holds our life vision precisely - impacting positively or negatively upon us. Rather like a powerful magnet- it provides a polarity to activate your life purpose and life vision. Where we live and work can awaken and expand us and our life vision into the world. The energy of where we live can awaken us to who we are and to that which we need to awaken in self to activate powerful life vision. What we need to transform and transcend in self will surface. Exactly who we are and the potential of who we are will increasingly surface.

It is an important time to consider just where you live and how this enhances your life vision. Are you energised? Are you inspired to create? Where are you inspired - not only to live but to work? Certain world locations will empower and radiate your life vision further into the world. Other locations will not and will fragment your life vision. It is important to note the way people are waking up to where they should live and work and are acting upon it. The quality of life vision is key.

Let's take a talented engineer born in Ghana as an example. He was living and trained in the UK with a PhD scholarship. He came for a life vision session to answer his questions on where he should live to maximise his potential. What became clear in the session was that his life vision lay in Africa - working in the oil industry with his already established network of professional engineers. He confirmed that prior to living in the UK, he had worked in the oil industry in Africa. This network would then lead him into creating environmental and community-based projects that would eventually lead him into politics in Ghana. As I keyed into the UK, the opportunities for him lay with research and teaching. He was unfulfilled and disappointed that he could not reach his potential in the UK.

Another example is of a vibrant American business woman working in the city in London who was facing burnout. She desperately wanted another child. She had faced miscarriage yet she desperately wanted success in her career as well. She and her family were based in the Home Counties. What became very clear, as I accessed her life vision, was a move to the east coast of North America. Deep down, she desperately wanted to live on the coast and to work from home in what would be a successful transfer of her existing career to working from home with assistants in other cities. Her quality of life would be improved by spending time with her family and focussing on having another child. She also wanted to balance her work life with writing and this she would achieve there.

In life vision sessions, I am aware that a person's life purpose can be crucially kick-started by living in certain, vital world locations. I see people exhausted in cities where they feel lost and directionless. I also see people alive, vibrant and in powerful life vision in cities. There is no formula except what awakens our life vision and where we resonate.

An Australian woman, working and living in London, came for a life vision session. As I worked, it became apparent that she desperately needed to return to Australia. London was not supporting her life vision in any way. In Australia, she would work with the environment with a focus on alternative tourism that would really allow visitors to tap into beautiful Australia. She was also deeply regretting leaving her soulmate as she hadn't had the courage to love him before. She confirmed that she was returning to Australia to focus upon this project that would inspire her for life. Everything I accessed about Australia totally resonated with her - the country, the land, the people, her love and her potential in work. London in no way could be this. She had to live and work in London to really awaken to her powerful life vision and just who she really is.

This is an exciting time when more people will understand their role as *creator* for self and the modern world. How many people are you hearing say, " I must take more responsibility for my self and what I create in my life" "The reactions and perceptions I have are very quickly manifesting in the world around me." "I must organise just what I do and who I am much more consciously."? There is an emerging global vision where we are being awakened to our power as a creator. We can consciously experience and create more in the modern world. This is an era (2007 to 2025) when so much more can be achieved not only as individuals, but for humanity and the world. As a new world vision unfolds- we are assessing the true nature and reality of what we have created so far- for self and world vision perspectives- we are awakening to moving beyond the *limited I*. From 2007- as the new world vision is awakened- one that is powerfully merging authenticity- and a deep vision of divinity- that moves beyond what we have known before. It is this deep authenticity- this deeper sense of divinity- a powerful knowing of truth- that is driving your awakening to consciously create a new vision of self and the world. Individuals are awakening in their vision of authentic life purpose. Individuals are expanding their life vision into the world. Vision becomes a spontaneous reality as we transform consciousness and energy to create. We expand into conscious creation. We are more aware of self- yet freed from the *limited I* and excuses of only me, me, me, I am not aware! The key here- is expansion- into the *infinite I*- where deepest authentic self discovery is key. The illusion of ME falls away. In all that you connect and create you recognise this expanded vision of who you are- it reminds you that all you connect with in life- is a deep reminder- of your authentic self- the divine self- the *infinite I*- and a constant reminder of who you truly are and your life purpose. 2007 to 2025 we are expanding into one vision- one vision for self and the world- truth- and from that expansion into consciously creating a new self and world vision that truly heals and transforms.

The focus is upon balance and anchoring new energies, consciousness qualities and life power tools so that we can transform self and world vision. The focus is upon awakening, energising, healing, and creating new self and world vision. So again - it is vital to know who we are and what our life vision is. In 2007 to 2025- we have the opportunity to create a vibrant world vision and to awaken to the role of humanity as conscious creator and powerful healer. What will be important is how we emerge as a group dynamic to achieve new world vision. Again, returning- to the concept of one vision- the *infinite I* will allow this expanding perspective and understanding self all that you connect and create. The I becomes more powerful than ever before- and perhaps we are awakening our divine power in the vision and creation of our destiny.

Isobel, through the Life Vision programme, transformed her confidence which had been sorely tried by an ex-husband who had reinforced so little sense of her power. She had an incredible healing journey and discovered her own power. This resulted in meeting her present husband, giving birth to a wonderful son and moving into business as a Shiatsu healer which she was able to do with balancing a home life.

Take a woman in her 30s as another example. Her life vision sessions confirmed her love of fashion and business. A successful wife, mother and career woman already - this project would not be a purely fashion-focussed venture. The life vision session included her love for her home and family - with work being located near home. The focus would be lifestyle with timeless beautiful clothes including beauty, styling, colour, life vision and nutrition.

This example highlights the potential of merging previously unrelated areas - focusing upon fashion and yet living and honouring one's self. The focus here is also about achieving more - for self and for others - in a creative business vision that is truly people-focussed. The exciting challenge is *being*. Perceiving that spirituality is *not* bound in meditation or within spiritual schools is key. It is an active and creative spirituality bound in the modern world. The concept of the *union* of ideas and ideals is being developed so that worlds merge dynamically to create a new individual and a world vision that will pioneer change.

The following is a very contemporary case study. A conventional man, mid-30s, visited me for a life vision session. He had never had a psychic reading. I explained to him that I would be working for the hour as a channel accessing his life vision and potential within the context of his major life areas. He was intelligent and challenging and was interested in what precise information would be accessed. His story absolutely embodies where we are now - as individuals striving to make that leap into dynamic world vision; the way that we are all searching for truth and a modern spirituality within our lives.

The life vision session connected with his potential both as an individual and globally with business development in both the private and public sectors. He had the potential to work with business development as a consultant. He would also work with maximising people potential within the workplace emphasising effective staff development. This was very important to him. His soul energy connected him immediately with Archangel Michael - drawing leadership qualities in business with strong and dynamic mental level ability that would ensure success. He had his own business. The future decade would link him to a very close family male connection in the United States with a business associated with computing. This would link him with software development in his expert area - business management and marketing. The pioneering software package would be global. The man was very surprised as the 'soul reading' precisely described his work and his link with the States was his best man, who was like a brother, who owned a computer company.

What the life vision session outlined were the qualities this man would develop to make the leap into powerful life and global vision. Power and leadership. Strong mental level and psychological expertise that he would bring to his understanding of people at work and home. High levels of spiritual and humanitarian awareness in the workplace so that he could maximise business productivity in companies and motivation in the workforce. All of these qualities would be expressed in an entirely practical way through work and home. The county of Surrey would bring him to exactly the right location to support his work, family and his social life. He and his family had just moved there! All of this information was required so that he could understand his quest for discovering modern spirituality in his life that encompassed work, home, his family, friends and his global vision. The session also embraced a great sense of his power and his potential to succeed in the UK, America and globally. This case study highlights the potential of individual spiritual vision and business fusing successfully in the modern world. A work/life balance! Another example of expanding life vision- and the power to achieve more.

It also reflects our increasing ability to create authentic life and global vision whilst balancing our hearts and minds, workplace with home life, careers and our loved ones. It gives us an insight into how complex our lives have become and how capable we are as individuals to maximise perfection in modern life. As our high soul energy and soul qualities are downloaded and become integrated into daily reality, the body is energised; the mind is focussed; the emotions are balanced. Healing, synchronicity and insight become an every day reality. We become our own powerful creator and healer - easily connecting with levels of consciousness and insight as never before. With body and soul in union, the modern world becomes the matrix for expression of life vision and world vision. Our spirituality becomes focussed into the world. Our life purpose becomes the divine, driving force allowing you to understand and expand who you are in each facet of our lives. This is true modern spirituality that will create a powerful new world vision- where your purpose-takes on a unique role in the destiny of the world.

We can create and express *who we are* powerfully in the modern world with:

• **Empowered Sensitivity**

• **Conscious Creativity**

• **Authenticity**

• **Truth**

• **Expanding Vision and Understanding**

There is a fusion of conscious/unconscious, mind/heart with an intelligence that we radiate *who we are* from authentic power, union and creative vision. There is an awakening of individual and world consciousness, of knowing and understanding, that is so crucially important for life vision. Knowing and understanding our life purpose- we can step into the potential of all knowing, all understanding. We can begin to know who we are with incredible depth and reality both in self and the modern world.

It is a powerful *union* of conscious/unconscious, of soul/body, of heart/mind. The Awakening brings a fusion of polarities to awaken us to our potential - not being purely individual or materially focussed; not thinking purely spiritually; not being immobilised by sensitivity; not being limited by the mind. But *being* multi-dimensionally aware. Being aware that levels and dimensions are inter-connected and inter-energised. This reality is awakening in self and in the modern world now. This brings us into powerful unity- the authentic self- directing and expanding your life vision.

The Awakening, 2007-2025, is developing increased energy levels and awareness so transformation can take place in individual and world vision. We are accessing this information powerfully both intellectually and in the way that we feel. There is a deep awakening to truth- to what is truth for self and a new world vision. The result is that ideas can merge and visionary solutions are accessed because we have the capacity to understand and achieve more. We move into expanded self- the *infinite I-* and new world vision . How we think, feel and create is being awakened from that higher self. Creatively, intellectually, emotionally and physi- cally - it is an exciting time for advancing a conscious new world vision.

Life vision then becomes a powerful physical expression and our understanding accelerates the way we consciously radiate ourselves into the world. We become more conscious of our essence and perhaps our soul. Our life vision flows and combines with the most physical, yet maintains the power and essence of us at deepest levels. Life vision can become an expression of our highest ideals and understanding of self. World vision and the modern world, then- informs and inspires us to truly be who we are.

In powerful synchronicity- we awaken essential energy for advanced spirituality, intellectual and creativity concepts in the modern world. Our vision and energy of self rapidly expands so that we can understand and create more in terms of life and world vision. At this time, it is more than being conscious of life vision- but our life purpose dynamically activated into the modern world- being informed by world vision- awakening us to achieve more. To become more. *Who am I* can then be expanded into the modern world, *via our awakening* into home, relationships, career, health and our expanding life and world vision. This is the expanding vision of authentic self and the world

An example of this is a single woman in her 40s. She had trained as a healer but had suffered from chronic fatigue having been a teacher for many years. The Life Vision programme empowered her with a greater sense of who she is. For many years this woman had not honoured herself by being the dis-empowered healer. Every life experience had eroded her sense of self, especially in love and career. The life vision session encouraged her to really see her potential not only as a healer but as an individual who had to create a vibrant support network for herself. The programme highlighted her tendency to be in the role of emotional doormat for everyone. This woman is now transformed. Her support is the self-healing she accesses daily for herself and on-going psychotherapy that will lead her into training as a counsellor so that she can be an empowered healer.

Another example is that of a talented artist, living in London who is also a committed Reiki master, massage therapist and spiritual healer. Every step she took she faced difficulty in London. She applied for an Arts Therapy MA and was rejected. Her life vision session had always indicated Glastonbury, UK- this was where she belonged. She moved there in autumn 2006 and at the same time applied for another Arts Therapy MA that was successful. She admitted her heart and soul indicated exactly where she should be.

The following example highlights the transformation that can take place if we, as individuals, really face who we are. A powerful, South African man in his 20s, on all levels advanced for his years who had never had a life vision session before sat for the whole hour without a word, totally expressionless. The session outlined his capacity in business, working with marketing and politics to develop a framework for business between Africa and the rest of the world - particularly the USA. He was working in business development to anchor some of poorest areas in Africa with some of the most powerful American businesses. This man believed in himself. He had the power and intellectual capacity to achieve this. As I finalised the session, I asked if he had any questions. He replied, "Tell me what I don't already know. But tell me how I can be just like you." The session finished with issues around his overconfidence that could potentially impair his wonderful world vision. He admitted this flaw.

I think what the case study highlights is that no matter how deep we hide who we are, all truths are emerging. At this time, we have to face the authenticity of who we are. Anything that limits who we- is going to be transformed- whether we flow with it or not. This is key to life vision-awakening in to the *infinite I*.

We are being awakened to have more energy and awareness on all levels. To have greater authenticity so that we can powerfully recognise self and the world. It moves us out of the individual. Creative group dynamics and intelligent world vision purpose, intensifies who we are. This further awakens our life vision so that we can expand and contribute more to the modern world . We are expanding into recognising powerful consciousness that will awaken action. We are waking to consciousness that is infinite. It is a time of awakening that will accelerate how fast we create our life and global vision, especially in large groups that are power-fully aligned to self and world vision. Powerfully resonating individuals awaken dynamic and synchronised life and world vision will increase. Our purpose is more powerful, our life vision is more powerful, our connection with the world is more dynamic and transforming than ever before. Our authenticity is powerfully reinforced.

It is about stepping right outside of the box and expanding into the potential of resonating with more than ever before.

The most beautiful, yet unhappy, French woman in her 30s came to see me. Everything was wrong in her life. She said little except that she wanted to cry. London was wrong, her friends were wrong, her partner incorrect, her career limiting. What this example reflects is that people are waking and waking fast to what is wrong not in their lives but deep within self. Life Vision returns once again to awakening more of the authentic self. As I did the session it became very apparent that this individual was deeply creative and sensitive and really needed to be expanded as a fashion designer. She also had the capacity to learn about her power through a design business and to expand her work into France and Italy. The photography that she had studied would be used as a marketing tool. She needed to come alive through being creative every day. Her attitude towards her relationship would markedly improve with the potential of marriage and a child. London would then become a supporting environment and one she would come to love as a result of activating a powerful life vision.

Life vision may connect you with very different individuals from very different worlds. We are seeing a fusion of conventional and unconventional, of business and spirituality, of education and healing, of integrity and politics, of creativity and economics, and psychology and psychic as examples. Be open to the potential of how you can expand as you awaken your life vision.

A case study example that really embodies this was that of a French man in his 40s who lived in South Africa. He wanted to know where he had to live to really live his life purpose. This man was working tirelessly to heal Africa. The life vision session focussed on his motivation to achieve change and stability for Africa whilst working within African and world governments. His life vision session tapped into his potential and also the drawbacks he faced in difficult countries with unstable political infrastructures. It also outlined his belief in an ethical approach to working with the potential wealth of Africa in terms of fuel. His work was founded upon his belief that he could work with others to heal Africa. At the end of the session, he outlined his concerns over what an ordinary man he was but that he had to carry on with this life vision that brought him into contact with leading business and political figures that shape the world. This man was learning to become more than he ever imagined.

Our understanding of world vision deepens as we understand and absorb multi-world perspectives. We connect more fully to who we truly are and the modern world. We understand more fully other polarities within self and the world - connecting with a powerful world vision and intelligence that is waking us to be and create more than we ever imagined possible. This is when the true healing and transformation will take place. It is now 2007 to 2025.

CHAPTER 4

ARCHANGELS OF THE LIFE VISION PROGRAMME

What are Archangels?

Archangels are banks of infinite energy and consciousness that awaken powerful alchemy on all levels within us. We are not invoking the typical archangel image of New Age or religions. We are going to explore the concept of archangels as being effective in awakening our powerful consciousness. They are:

- the most powerful psychological alchemy tools

- the life power tools of vision

- the life power tools of creation

- the life power tools of healing

- the activating tools of *infinite I*

Archangels in the Life Vision programme are vast energy and information banks that can help us transform our deepest healing issues and activate the life power tools that awaken us into our empowered life vision and energy. The Awakening System helps us to activate   expansive soul qualities of the *infinite I* (examples are given below) which are essential for the creation of a dynamic life vision.

As a highly trained channel, I am able to locate and unlock empowered life purpose. I also locate and awaken your unique expansive soul qualities associated with key archangels that will ever power the *infinite I* into your life vision. Equally, I can track and locate healing issues essential for your awakening which can be rapidly transformed by harnessing particular archangel energy and information. This helps individuals to understand self and the world at significantly deeper expanding levels.

You, too, can begin to harness an infinite source of energy and information that can powerfully inform and create your life vision. You can learn to intelligently connect and awaken with one or more archangel. Within The Awakening System, it is important to explore each of the four archangels - Michael, Uriel, Gabriel and Raphael. Each one defines access to a higher authentic energy, vision, healing and our essential expansive soul qualities for activating empowered life and universal vision.

The Awakening System will teach you how to access archangels to awaken your life vision in powerful union of body and soul, mind and heart, self, the modern world and universe. This activates powerful alchemy on all levels. When every level informs there is no separation. Vision, creation, alchemy and healing are available every moment with synchronicity flowing. This is The Awakening or new world vision 2007 to 2025.

The key focus of The Life Vision programme is deep conscious understanding of your life purpose and your expanding power to achieve your life vision within the world once you step into the *infinite I*. The aim is conscious and creative modern spirituality. This is activated with modern visionary techniques that explore the four archangels from a new and very practical modern world perspective.

Archangel Michael - The Visionary ✗

Key concepts are: truth and empowerment.

Archangel Michael is the *Divine Power Source*. Michael is the divine visionary, architect and creator, awakening powerful insight and intelligence that can be transformed to the most material and physical levels. Michael is omnipresent.

Michael brings a powerful multi-dimensional awakening of who you are and your life vision. Michael defines purpose and authenticity - discovering and activating a powerful sense of purpose. Michael evokes responsibility and leadership for self, humanity and the world with precision focus and attention to detail. Michael activates an understanding within you - of divine and universal consciousness and your ability to expand and experience beyond self yet also within the most material and physical context.

Michael awakens great physical energy and the energy to achieve; to fulfil life vision. Michael represents humanity and world progression, progressive ideas, ideals and their powerful manifestation. Michael will expand your awareness, insight and infinite ability to heal and transform not only you and your life vision but your world vision.

As you channel Archangel Michael, your physical, emotional and intellectual levels will be understood at significantly deeper levels and powered to higher capacity and organisation therefore contributing more to humanity and world vision.

Michael anchors and focuses - allowing you to *be* in the modern world; to stand firmly in your life vision; to hold your life vision. You will activate immense power, strength and freedom and these will emerge as high soul qualities. The Awakening 2007 to 2025 opens knowledge in new directions; a fusion of the old and new. Michael emphasises world understanding and conscious action. Michael awakens self and humanity to these ideals.

Archangel Michael is the *visionary* for self and the world; drawing forward qualities to be still and yet powerfully active. Michael will develop within you the deepest insight to respond in action to ideas and ideals for self and the world. Michael awakens thinking and creation - a union between conscious intelligence and manifestation. This develops purpose.

Archangel Michael activates empowerment. Michael activates a psychological and emotional alchemy that is powerful - you awaken to being authentic on all levels.

You awaken multi-dimensional consciousness yet with power and intelligence to create. You become solid, strong, anchored fully in the world and humanity-focussed. Michael represents an infinite journey for understanding and transforming self - and using that intelligence consciously and creatively for self and the world.

You might like to consider the life power tools that Archangel Michael facilitates:

Limited Self/Healing Issues	Infinite I/Expansive Soul Qualities
Fear	Authentic Power
Doubt	Divine Power
Lack of purpose	Empowerment
Directionless	Expanding consciousness
Lack of focus	Direction
Lack of vision for self and the world	Modern Spirituality
Powerless	Flow
Stagnation	Precision focus
Problems around manifestation	Vision
Grounding issues	Conscious creation
Over-focus- thinking	Expansion
Over-focus- organising	Powerful action
Imbalance	Achievement
Over concern with responsibility	Organisation
Only material vision	The Visionary
Only spiritual vision	
Inaction	

Archangel Gabriel – The Creator ◯

Key concepts are: conscious creation
The power of the heart. The power of the earth heart. The power of the divine feminine heart. Archangel Gabriel awakens you to the emergence of the power of your heart that will allow you to feel truth in your body, taking you beyond what can be intellectualised into fully knowing. This moves you beyond consciously knowing and extends you into consciously feeling, consciously intuiting.

Archangel Gabriel will generate the power to heal, support, to communicate from the heart in highest levels of expression and awareness. The focus is upon the arts, culture, communication, languages, media, politics and world vision.

Gabriel expands a powerful sense of the healer and what healing can be - the dynamics of mother and child (what a relationship can be) and your relationship with earth and nature. Gabriel will empower you with confidence, balance, harmony, integrity and truth so that you can communicate exactly who you are in the modern world. The globe is a key image - representing healing through communication and language. It is a powerful time when language may be regarded with deeper meaning. Conscious use of language and listening will produce profound healing and hold a significantly more conscious humanity. Information is being expanded - the internet is a powerful physical manifestation of the way communication is expanding on all levels.

Conscious thought, intention and language are key and again empower the way you radiate who you are. Gabriel also reinforces an earth-focussed vision that anchors self, humanity and the world. Stability is key for humanity and the environment whilst activating high soul qualities and intelligence in the way we create world vision.

Consider the life power tools, Archangel Gabriel assists us with:

Limited I/Healing Issues	Infinite I/Expansive Soul Qualities
Lack of confidence	Divine feminine awakening
Self confidence	Confidence
Self acceptance issues	Heart centred-consciousness
Communication issues	Love/acceptance- self, humanity, the
Creative block	world
Self love issues	Creative and empowered communi-
Acceptance of others- the world	cation
High levels of sensitivity	Creativity
Lack of responsibility	Inspiration
Over-active sensitivity	Self love
Imagination- lack of anchoring into	Empowerment
the world	Creative and empowered sensitivity
Uncertainty	Responsibility
	Truth
	Integrity
	Imagination
	Authentic/divine connection to earth
	and world vision
	Healing
	The Divine Feminine Creator

Archangel Uriel – The Alchemist ▲

Key concepts are: Alchemy

Archangel Uriel awakens the power of the highest spiritual perspective - awakening consciousness and bringing freedom of the body, mind and emotional levels. Freedom is key – the highest perspective that creates freedom for self, humanity and the earth.

Uriel activates intelligence and powerful personal power so that you may intelligently and swiftly create your life. Uriel awakens the pioneer and forward thinking for self, humanity and the earth. Archangel Uriel brings the power of spiritual intelligence on all levels - creating a powerful and sensitive channel with multi-dimension perspective and vision. The key to Uriel is consciousness beyond humanity and the physical. High levels of sensitivity will awaken knowledge beyond what we already consciously know.

This archangel has a powerful empathy with the sun - with rapid transformation, manifestation, alchemy and the world. There is focus and dynamism - a powerful psychological yet spiritual perspective. It is important to note that Uriel will transform powerless into empowerment. Uriel will waken physical, emotional and mental level strength by truly awakening the power of the soul.

The soul is key with Uriel. This archangel awakens soul wisdom and the possibility that you can live with the highest spiritual ideals and activate these in the world. The perfectionist is key - meticulous attention to detail and truth that can be directed to business development, psychology and learning about the power of the mind. Uriel is the alchemist awakening esoteric knowledge.

The intensity of Uriel brings superb independence and self-empowerment with the power to achieve. The dynamic drive to transform self, humanity and the world with new world vision is key.

Life power tools that Archangel Uriel facilitates:

Limited I/Healing Issues	Infinite I/Expansive Soul Qualities
Fear of sensitivity	Empowered sensitivity
Fear of people	Power of advanced consciousness
Fear of darkness	High healing sensitivity and ability
Acute psychic sensitivity	Psychic sensitivity- empowered
Powerless	Emotional neutrality/balance
Inability to focus, ground or anchor	Empowerment
High spiritual perspective incom-	Discipline- physical, emotional, intel-

patible with the modern world

Future focussed

Manifestation issues

Emotional imbalance

Detachment

Isolation

Lack of stamina- physical, emotional, intellectual

lectual, spiritual

Focus, anchoring, grounding

High spiritual perspective-empowered

High levels of physical energy

Awareness of own power and the ability to galvanise transformation on all levels

Synchronicity- high levels of energy

Power on all levels

Acceptance of self, humanity and the world

Freedom

The alchemist, transformation, power to achieve

Insight- world vision

Archangel Raphael – The Infinite Healer ●

Key concepts: powerful healing and expansion.

Archangel Raphael invokes clear perspective of who you are and your position within the universe - focussing upon the physical and universal, you awaken complete perspective of the power of who you are and your infinite divinity. You awaken to understanding precisely how universal energies and information can inform you of who you are. This can awaken significant multi-dimension awareness and the ability to transcend time and space. Raphael invokes a sense of future potential realities. The stillness Raphael invokes allows a deep yet expansive vision and a sense of self that allows you freedom from fear. You will know and understand a 'you' who is aware of a wider world and universal vision. Raphael allows you to experience beyond every day, beyond self in limited consciousness.

Raphael awakens deepest joy and comedic insight into the questions of our relationship with the world and universe. Raphael awakens intense channelling ability so that you can harness universal consciousness. Order is key for self, humanity, the world and universe. Archangel Raphael activates understanding of the inter-dimension matrixes. You awaken consciousness that travels at speed and with precision. Mental agility and stillness is key with Raphael. Raphael awakens you to the power of the mind to transform and invent self. Raphael awakens the newest ideas. Because Raphael delivers you the freedom to experience self, the world and the universe, your world instantly expands allowing potential and opportunities to rapidly be achieved. With stillness, you can manifest. With expansion, you can achieve more. You begin to flow. You are aware of the power of inter-connectedness in everything. You become aware of the fabric and structure of the universe. You become aware that energy is thought, with each thought being realised at every level.

Archangel Raphael helps with awakening these life power tools:

Limited I/Healing Issues	Infinite I/Expansive Soul Qualities
Restlessness	Stillness
Lack of connection with the world	Peace
Lack of body focus and connection with the world	Centeredness
	At one
Hyper-sensitivity	Knowing
Fear of the world	Acceptance
High spiritual values and ideals	The new divine plan for humanity and
Pain and extreme suffering sensitivity	the world
Lack of flow between ideas and the	Pioneering spiritual development and
modern world	awareness
Lost connection with soul and divinity	Empowered new energy- especially
	indigos

Infinite light and healing
The power and freedom of
consciousness
All knowing
The freedom to be

Awakening

Essential Foreword

It is essential to create the self space and self focus before you begin any Life Power exercises in this book.

Centring Self

Find a suitable space to start the exercise. A calm space, a space in nature- whatever supports who you are. 5 minutes.

You ideally should be seated- alert in the body and mind yet relaxed and peaceful. It is this polarity that is very important so that you easily access information without falling asleep! It is essential- the physical body awakening to new levels of energy and insight- key in transforming your energy base so that you can create more from the divine self and radiate into the modern world.

Take five deep breaths. Focus on the feet , the legs, the body, head, arms and hands. Focus up through the spine and into the brain. Now focus into your heart. As you create focus into the body deepen the breath. This will expand your awareness quickly. Spend several minutes in this exercise.

Visualise light (sunlight) expanding from the feet through your body into your head. The physical body containing this light

Now you are centred.

Expansion

After following the first exercise you are ready to work with expansion.

5 minutes.

Press your feet into the floor. Expand in light by visualising it all around you and focus it within you especially from your spine, heart and head. Expand this into your feet and into your hands

Focus light radiating from your heart and head. Feel and visualise the connection between your heart and mind. Visualise a diamond of light in your heart connecting a diamond of light in the centre of your brain.

Visualise and expand a diamond of light in the crown of your head.

Take five deep breaths. Energise and radiate more light. Continue pressing your feet into the floor- so that the body is anchoring this expansion.

Open Your eyes. This will powerfully awaken you and expand insight.

Closing

This is essential in all Life Power exercises for integration of new levels of self, insight, healing and energy. 5 minutes.

Upon finishing an exercise or exercises. Take five deep breaths. Slow your focus right into the physical body. Take your focus into the head, body, arms, hand, legs and feet. Slowly work into each area. Visualise how expanded you are and consciously tighten your focus right into the body. You may visualise expanded light all around you- now pull that into the physical body.

You are closed.

Activating Archangels

You can activate the archangels as follows: **name and symbol.**

X Michael visualise as two triangles of light. The apex to apex meeting in your heart and ?expanding powerfully from the heart.

○ **Gabriel** visualise as a sphere of light

▲ **Uriel** as a triangle of light expanding from the centre of your heart so that the triangle surrounds you.

● **Raphael** as a point of light held in your heart.

Exercise to channel one of the Archangels

Sit comfortably. Focus into the body. Work with Centring and Expansion exercises first.

Take five deep breaths. You will first focus into your heart. Visualise light in your heart. Expand this vision. Focus into the brain. Visualise light in the brain. Expand this vision.

In all of the Life Power exercises your aim is to awaken new levels of energy and insight. In developing precision focus- you also powerfully expand and energises who you are.

This exercise can be applied to each archangel and used in the same way to awaken who you are. Focus upon one of the archangels.

For example, archangel Michael. ▐

Take five deep breaths. Expand in light from within and radiating all around you. Begin consciously connecting to Michael by using name and visualising symbol from the heart. As you enter the exercise more deeply through precision focus and the breath expand the symbol up and down. Expansion is key so expand. You will feel powerfully connected with your body, heart and mind. Awakened.

Take five deep breaths. Powerfully connecting with archangel Michael.

The more you deepen your experience of this exercise through heart and mind, the more you will consciously connect with archangel Michael. You will begin to activate Life Power tools. You will begin to expand the Infinite I and expanding soul qualities. Refer to archangel Michael, page 29

Take five breaths and press your feet into the floor.

Open your eyes. You may wish to draw or write what you have

experience. Further insight can be gained.

Keep a Journal

Write down what you have experienced or information that you have channelled.

What expanding soul qualities did the Archangel bring?

How do you feel?

What do you need to transform?

What do you feel inspired to create in self and the modern world?

Use Archangel Michael to transform any healing issues you have

For example (archangel Michael, page 44): low physical energy to energised, vibrant, focussed energy or fear to confidence and strength

Awakening the Power of Archangels Michael and Gabriel ✗ ○ ✝

This is a powerful exercise. See a sphere of light all around you. Within that sphere is a cross of radiant white light.

As you begin to channel Michael, sense the power of Michael working down through your energy field as the vertical in the cross. See the energy as radiant white.

Really connect into just what Archangel Michael represents - the high soul qualities - and feel the energy and information being channelled through you on all levels.

Press your feet into the floor and take five deep breaths. Deepen the breath to deepen the channelling. Hold the vision of Michael.

Now draw upon the power of Gabriel as the horizontal in the cross. See the energy as radiant white.

Take five deep breaths. Connect with name and symbol of Gabriel. Press your feet into the floor. Expand this symbol all around you.

Consciously connect with what Gabriel represents.

Connect with archangel Michael - vertical - and Gabriel - horizontal - so that you have a radiant white cross within the sphere of light you have created around you.

Take five deep breaths. Spend five to ten minutes in precision focus and expanding this visualisation. This will heal and transform you. This will also focus you and connect powerfully with self and the world.

Press your feet into the floor.

Open your eyes.

You can write down your experience to consolidate the channelling and healing.

This is a particularly important and powerful exercise as it awakens your power and ability to communicate just who you are.

Awakening the Power of Uriel and Raphael ▲ ● ✝

This exercise will awaken and expand the vision of who you are with expansive insight and high levels of new energy.

Sit comfortably. Press your feet into the floor. Close your eyes.

Take five deep breaths. See a sphere of light all around you. Within that sphere is a cross of radiant white light.

Visualise Uriel vertically as light down through the head and heart. Consciously connect with name Uriel.

Expand Raphael as light horizontally from the heart.

Press your feet into the floor.

Take five deep breaths and focus and expand ▲ ● for five to ten minutes - consciously expanding and exploring these two archangels within your sphere of light.

You can write down your experience to consolidate the channelling and healing.

Awakening The Divine Power of Four Archangels

We can achieve a powerful union of the masculine and feminine within-awakening body and soul, heart and mind. This will translate powerfully into your vision of self, world and universe.

For example. With Michael as the divine masculine and Gabriel, as the divine feminine ?

A powerful union and symbolism that takes you into conscious awakening and conscious creation of who you are. Taking you into being infinitely healing. This takes you into all knowing- in mind and heart. The visionary and the creator in all that you are.

For example. With Uriel and Raphael in powerful union and symbolism ?

I have newly discovered the importance in awakening the divine power of working with these two archangels in awakening new world vision that deepens our perspective of who we are both spiritually and universally. Almost awakening self to truly contribute more to the world than ever before. This powerfully awakens the alchemist and infinite healer. This also awakens new and empowered energy levels essential in the transition into *infinite I*. You will experience a shift in consciousness and a new, more powerful energy base for self and humanity. This takes us into authentic self, divine self- discovery and expansion. This takes us into fully understanding consciousness as a tool to fully understand who we truly are.

CHAPTER 5

DISCOVERING WHO YOU ARE

"I came from a very ordinary and not too well-to-do family in the West Riding of Yorkshire comprising of my mother, father, younger brother and me. I had to leave grammar school around my 16th birthday because my father died and my mother was ill, and I joined the local council as an articled pupil civil engineer, almost the last of these. After about 6 years of this I went to university and got a degree in civil engineering, a profession I continued in for a total of around 14 years. I then moved sideways into the Water Industry. It was a very high profile job within the international water sector and I lived a very intensive life, trying to balance job with family life, with 2 small children, a boy and a girl. One day in 2001, I looked around me and asked myself "is this all there is?" and decided to quit, doing so in 2002. After all the exhilaration, that sort of life had become an anti-climax and I had gone as far as I could in that career line. I also felt, without being able to pin it down, that there were other things I should be doing.

I left to become a consultant/writer on international water policy, strategy and management with global clients. I have been able to capitalise on my reputation, contacts, knowledge and skills to work on some high profile projects. I regard myself as a relatively humble man, despite the heights I reached – fame and fortune have not really been my main motivators. I also spent a year training as a garden designer although, because of the water work, I have done little of this.

I have always been interested in matters esoteric and occult since I was a teenager and had read widely on all aspects of them, becoming a member of the Arcane School in London in 1991/2. It provides a distance learning programme comprising of guided self-study, meditation (always on a seed thought) and service work. The work has a strong theoretical content which is highly intellectual (text books include those by Helen

Blavatsky and Alice Bailey). It was very difficult to measure what spiritual progress I was making since there were few clues although I feel the programme brought me enormous benefits and to others also. I came across the College of Psychic Studies and decided to have a psychic consultation. I was drawn to Tracey because of her emphasis on 'life purpose', which I had long felt I had not really identified and was feeling restless about, particularly, and also soul contracts. I met her in early summer 2005, had the reading and have since done a number of workshops and courses."

Tony

I had no knowledge of Tony before meeting him for his life vision session. The session took place in 2005.

" You are very strongly questioning spirituality and Theosophy. As I channel Archangel Michael, you have a great sense of the need to maintain balance. A real period of not knowing which way to go - you are learning not to doubt who you are. This can cause you to be ungrounded.

Landscape design makes you strong and masterful, connecting you with the land and honouring the environment. Translate spiritual teachings in this way. Spiritual awareness will be brought through your surroundings in nature and water. Land, nature, water; how you use your existing skills to create harmony in nature and the world; this will be more commercial and more home-focussed. Once you get the space around you correct, the landscape, then you will achieve in writing. You will have symmetry on all levels. Connecting with solid earth energies and writing more spiritually on the environment - concerning the earth - how we treat it. You are creating your perfection first (with self and at home) then you will feel comfortable with writing - with the emphasis upon *the balance of the earth* - the theoretical and the meditative. Concepts like whether we

should support the globe or not, whether we let the earth fall or not. Your writing will be pivotal and important. It has wider implications - it is not industry-based. You will relax into this and it will be accessible to people on an everyday basis. You will then have peace within."

"I trained as a garden designer last year!"
" I was director of an international water foundation!"

"Your relationship with your wife - she anchors you in the most practical sense. She can completely embrace who you are and at the same time you are infuriating. Your ideas can become your passion. You both have home strongly within your pathways. A lot of you is surrendering to your spirituality at home - your landscape design project is anchoring you both.

The answers are here. Create a channel - to write - linked with the earth and water. This work will open doors in working with the environment. Create a dialogue with higher spiritual levels. You are a visionary in terms of the way you see the earth's development. New thinking in terms of working with water. Learn to channel to write. As your writing grows, your work is evolving in the next three years. Your writing will be contemporary and mainstream. This work will take you into a public domain. Your soul purpose concerns the way we are holding the earth, in the way the balance of the earth rests in our hands.

You are interested in educating people. This links you into everything you have learned - your passion in a practical way - the way that people think and feel about the earth. Your work is long term in the next ten to fifteen years. It is what real people need - not taking it to academics but to real people! You have the power to talk to charities with important work in other countries. This is how you will make it more and more real. You will learn how to articulate what

you have learned...expressing your spiritual integrity to a whole network of people."

This is what Tony said about his life vision session and life vision programme.

"Tracey's work is very different to most of what I have done before - very practical, down to earth and immediate. Is there anything stronger, more centring and motivating than to know what one's life purpose is? For me it is hard to think so, but I have always, all my life, been focussed on work. For long years I have sought to know more about my life purpose and Tracey's reading is the only time I have ever had meaningful insight into it. Life seems more harmonious, including family life. The whole business of spiritual development seems a lot more practical than before."

Tony is a powerful contemporary case study. He highlights modern spiritual issues around living life purpose and being in powerful life vision. Tony had a life vision session at an important time in his life. Already with a widely regarded and successful career, he was unfulfilled. He was unfulfilled at home and unfulfilled spiritually. Tony had strongly intellectualised everything - to the point that nothing could be free to flow into his life. Tony was trying to achieve in his home, work and relationships. He had amassed too much knowledge and responsibility, preventing him from true inspiration and the wisdom of his heart and soul.

This century brings new awakening for each one of us - how do we achieve perfect polarisation of the mind and heart, the soul and physical? The demands are greater – the vision more perfect - we are entering a new era in modern spiritual awakening and vision.

Tony has now embarked upon a powerful spiritual approach to his life and his work with water and focussing on writing a book and educating a wider audience on global water environmental issues.

Who am I and what is 'spirituality'?

These are really important concepts to address. Who am I? Just what is spirituality? How do we really express spirituality consciously?

An exercise to help discover 'Who Am I?'

Connect first with Archangel Michael.

Sitting comfortably. Press your feet into the floor. The Awakening System works with expansion and focus at all times - so stay awake in your body, heart and mind. Be alert and vibrant.

Take five deep breaths.

The aim is to awaken on all levels in precision focus.

Take five deep breaths and be aware of your body. See white light expanding from your feet all the way through your body to your head. Be conscious of focussing this light right inside your physical body. See a pyramid of light all around you.

Take another five deep breaths and continue pressing your feet into the floor.

Stay focussed upon this vision for a few minutes. You are activating your soul and its light. Be conscious of your body.

Connect with the energy of Archangel Michael. (The power of your meditation comes from working towards conscious connection with all levels yet knowing your own centre.)

Take five deep breaths – connecting further with Archangel Michael. Allow Archangel Michael's energy to encompass you and absorb the healing and information. Explore this.

This is a powerful exercise - Michael is key to spirituality, both under-standing and practical.

Use this exercise daily to align you with a deep sense of purpose. Allow yourself the time to integrate the energies and information after this meditation by focussing into the body, down through the brain, into spine, into fingertips, into feet. Pull your expanded energy field right into your body. Take a few minutes, in silence, to absorb all the information received.

Archangel Michael - channelled by Tracey Ash, 2006.

" Michael brings forward intense light, healing, divine and humanitarian wisdom to direct the way, your way. Michael brings the greatest mental clarity and vision for self and others. This quality of light, of consciousness and of vision is key. With Archangel Michael there is freedom from all self-limitations and fear. With Michael comes the deepest focus, conscious creation and responsibility for self and others. Universal and divine awareness may be drawn upon so that you know your life purpose. You know who you are and your life vision in the most practical and conceptual ways.

Michael will empower you to know who you are and the potential of what you can achieve. The deepest spiritual understanding can be activated with the power to translate that into the physical body and material levels. Michael will considerably increase your physical energy levels and transform you by healing. You will organise and achieve more. This archangel can provide the energetic framework for your life purpose to be activated - empowering and energising the body, balancing and focussing the heart and mind and activating higher soul levels. Archangel Michael inspires a deep responsibility for humanity and the direction of humanity and with this you can align your life purpose to a significant global vision. "

Make a list of what inspires you

This exercise will help you to access your own spirituality.

Write down what you feel in your life inspires and resonates with you. Is it the theatre, ballet, music, art, healing, bodywork, nature, sculpture, meditation, politics, people, learning, creating, teaching, even a location in the world?

Make a list and continually update it. See this list as an expression of your spirituality. See the world as an expression of your spirituality and just how energising the world can be!

Through using this list, you will remember, expand and energise who you truly are.

It is important to actively work with your list to inspire a powerful and creative life vision. Take one activity and really absorb it into just who you are. **Be it! Do it!** This allows profound healing to take place as you awaken to infinite healing available within the world.

An exercise awaken your Life Purpose
Take five deep breaths. Pressing your feet into the floor, gain body awareness - being conscious is key. You can work with a body-focus for anchoring or grounding for a few minutes. Allow light to flow through you and around you.

Expand from your heart centre as a powerful diamond of light. Let the diamond surround you.

Focus on this vision for 3 – 5 minutes.

Take another five deep breaths.

Visualise a diamond of light in the centre of your head - allowing the diamond of light to expand and connect with your heart.

Focus on this visual for 3 – 5 minutes.

Ask the question: What is my Life Purpose? Return to that question throughout the meditation.

Take five deep breaths. You may wish to channel Archangel Michael to deepen your life vision and anchor the information within you by remaining conscious and focussed for about five minutes.

Now write down the information you received. Write down what feelings, pictures, thoughts you've received. You will receive more information as you write so continue working with this exercise on a daily basis to inform and energise you.

CHAPTER 6

HEALING YOUR SELF

"I was born on the 14th July 1974 in Bucks England. Two weeks later I was put up for adoption.

After about a year of different foster parents I was adopted by a couple with a 5 year old daughter. We travelled a lot as a family and I spent a mainly happy if somewhat misunderstood childhood living between Europe and the United States.

When I was 16, things started to change and the next 10 years would prove to be very difficult for me. First my mother was diagnosed with inoperable brain cancer and after a brief struggle of five weeks, died in the summer of 1990. I left home soon after this and was a year later diagnosed HIV+. Being told at 17 that I had 10 years maximum to live was my first wake up call, but I saw it as an excuse to live fast and die young. Around my 19th birthday my father told me he also had cancer and by the time my 21st birthday came he was in hospital. The week he died I received a letter from my boyfriend's parents in Israel telling me that he had lost his battle with AIDS and was also dead.

At 21 I felt very alone in the world. After this I went all out to destroy myself with clubs, drugs and bad living. I had watched three of the most important people in my life suffer and die and I wanted to go suddenly, without pain.

When combination therapy was introduced I had to re-learn how to live again. I stumbled through various drug re-habs, unsuccessful combinations and immune collapses until I was diagnosed with cancer in 2002. This really did It - the disease that killed both my parents was now growing inside me. "Just cut it out", I told my doctor and he did, but when he told me that I needed chemo and radio therapy I refused - no way was I going to go through that. There had to be another way to beat this and regain my health. I had realized when I found the lump that I had a choice - live or die. It was make your mind up time. I also knew that if I chose to live I had to wake up this time and really find out why I was here...

By the time I got to Tracey, despite the combination therapy, my health was still deteriorating with the HIV as the opportunistic development of testicular cancer showed. Mentally I was in shock. I also had a lot of fear - not so much of death, as I had been expecting that for years, more of the suffering that I had seen others go through before death comes. I was under a lot of pressure from my doctors to undergo radio and chemo therapy as follow-up to the removal of the tumour r- which had turned out to be a particularly virulent form of sarcoma. I needed answers, and fast..."

Tony

Tony came for a life vision session in summer 2002. He was desperate for healing. He had had readings with many sensitives, psychics and mediums. He felt largely misunderstood by any of them. All told them that he was on the right pathway. Tony knew differently. His health was now also being affected. His immune system was breaking down. He also had cancer. His session was one of the most memorable in terms of healing and empowerment for a client. It was an honour and privilege to work with such an incredible man. He needed help very quickly.

The life vision session turned around his attitudes and his approach to his life. It encouraged a great awakening of his power and life changes that would revolutionise his health.

When I interviewed Tony in 2004, I had no idea of what impact the information had had on his life and health. I shall be very clear that the information in this session was important in Tony's life healing because it opened his awareness of his own power to change his life and heal himself. I would like to stress that it is important to be aware that the work we did brought a framework to support the treatment he was receiving from medical professionals.

This is his story of how I helped him to discover that the power to heal was within him,

" In January 2002 I'd been living with HIV for 10 years when I developed cancer. At this point, instead of giving up, I started asking myself 'what is this for and why now?'

Tracey explained that I was not saying 'yes' to life. I needed to develop myself - heal on an emotional level- and gain my power and embrace my spirituality. My body was taking the brunt of me not getting on with my life purpose. Tracey told me that my diet was directly affecting my health and that I CAN HEAL MYSELF. I was told that I am a natural healer who was healing those around me but not using this gift for myself.

It was a huge turning point in my life when I understood what I must do. I had never considered working with spirit and although I had been told that I was a healer before, had always considered myself too sick to be of any use to anyone.

I am sure that if it weren't for the information given to me through Tracey, my health would have continued to deteriorate from an already dangerously bad place. As it is, I've been clear of cancer for 2 years now and my overall health is far better than it's been in years and getting better all the time! I received a huge amount of healing in the initial reading - that I now recognise was on all levels.

Having a purpose and direction to follow was very important to me at that stage in my life, and the reading gave me both. For the first time in my life I felt I was beginning to understand why I was here and felt able to get on with my true journey.

The information from the session in June 2002 was all so relevant. My health was suffering and was an indication of me saying 'no' to life in the physical. I was suffering in a dramatic way - a dramatic loss of weight, no energy and I had cancer. Since honouring my spirit, my strength and health has gone from strength to strength. I have turned any negative issues around. I have put on weight. I have been clear from any kind of cancer for nearly 2 years. I am so much more balanced. I have healing. I am starting to want my life. I have changed my attitude towards the world and to my soul purpose.

Believe me, I had lots of readings and everyone said that I was on the right path but Tracey gave me very different information that I needed to hear and I am very grateful to her. I didn't just listen to the reading. I listened to the reading for over a year. The information and events she gave me happened very organically and in synchronicity.

By 2003 I began training as a healer on the Healing Accreditation Course at The College of Psychic Studies. In 2004 I began to start healing clients. Within two years of the reading in June 2002, all of the information has manifested or is manifesting. I now also work for The Samaritans."

Here are parts of Tony's session. I had no previous connection with Tony nor knowledge of his life story.

" Sometimes it is very difficult for you to find where you fit into life. You need to feel like you belong. You have very good communication skills. Training in counselling would help you to ground through the mental level. Continue with your own personal counselling work as well. You are looking to create a balance between the spiritual, psychic, mental, emotional and physical levels.

Your way of being is very cerebral. The focus of your life is upon your power, strength and your ability to heal and transcend old selves. You are very childlike. You don't feel like being here. You are restless internally. You need to turn that very dynamic energy into creativity. You need to learn how to work with your intuitive and intellectual abilities.

In terms of self, you need to heal on an emotional level and regain personal power.

Heal your sensitivity. Embrace your spirituality. You need to learn about your power. You can at times fear trespassing other peoples' emotions. It can be quite painful for you to enter into other peoples' energy fields. This is powerful. You are looking at your compassion for humanity and self rather than criticise. You must overcome your doubt, as you fear the worst outcome for yourself. You need to turn around what being intuitive is - be positive. You are drawn to very ancient forms of spirituality. You need stillness and space around yourself. You are still craving that stillness, control and isolation. Reclaim this power as positive.

This lifetime you will work with people, drawing upon intuitive and healing energies. Not taking your personal power is affecting your physical health. It is affecting your immune system. Not connecting with your soul purpose is affecting your body.

Your mother was very depressed when you were a child. She tried to shape you through her own fears. She found it difficult to handle you. There have been so many times when you have decided that you haven't wanted to be here."

Tony confirmed that he had found himself trying to commit suicide as a young child.

"Your health is related to you not being grounded. You are a natural channel but you have not taken your power in it. You need to be empowered by your sensitivity and transcend the wounded inner child. You need to work with healing. You need to develop as a healer.

In terms of your health, there is a breakdown in the immune system. The eyesight is being affected. These physical problems will clear. You are leaving little energy for yourself. You also feel fragmented. There is a struggle between masculine and feminine energies. There is conflict, angst, fear, doubt and depression. There is a cycle of returning to childhood. You were a very imaginative and

creative child- reconnect with that. Your will has been broken. Eastern traditions will help strengthen you - mantras, silent meditations, working with your voice. Your voice will change and deepen. The virus attacking your immune system (he confirmed aids and cancer) **requires energy healing every week. You are learning how to heal and manage self. As your energy changes, a non-dairy diet will help you resonate on a purer vibration. In all, you will be healing self and moving from your fears to working and healing others. Those people will be aids clients, people who are struggling. You will be counselling."**

What we can learn from Tony here is not only incredible compassion for his journey of self-discovery that took him in many directions until he awakened, but finding the deeper courage to really connect with self. At one time or another, each one of us could be deeply afraid of connecting with and discovering just who we are. In Tony's case, his life vision was in chaos - his true self unheard. He was directionless and lacking in essential life-force energy to heal and inspire himself forward.

Tony is an extremely powerful example: his dis-ease affirming the fragmentation of self. He was allowing himself to be dis-empowered. The experience of serious illness allowed him to meet his power, to recognise his power in the most transformational and healing way. He discovered no single person could heal him. He learned to discover and heal himself.

I feel Tony is an important example of our time - there is a major awakening shift that is allowing each one of us to recognise our power and become our own healer. It is about surrendering to and being supported by every dimension, and anchoring into the modern world. Tony found day-to-day existence very difficult because of his sensitivity so he hit the self-destruct button. So much of his life vision, his life purpose is bound in self-discovery and healing and, once he recognised this, healing could take place.

The deepest sense of self is being activated. To awaken consciously at the deepest emotional levels to the expansion and speed of the higher mind you can develop dynamic inspiration, creative vision and the power to achieve transformation for self and the world. This is a time (2007 to 2025) of boundless potential when we break down any limits we have placed upon ourselves in terms of what the mind can experience and achieve.

Powerful Healing Affirmations

* I honour who I am

* I am powerfully anchored in my life

* I am powerful

* I am healing myself

Life Vision Programme
1. *The Diamond.*
Sit comfortably and take five deep breaths.

Visualise the most exquisite diamond. You can see it - very small at first. Sunlight expands this diamond, allowing it to sparkle to life. See it and feel it expanding as a multi-coloured rainbow.

Take five deep breaths. Press your feet into the floor. The most radiant sunlight is flowing through your body. See and sense your heart and mind being powerfully energised. Your diamond is holding you. It is all around you. YOU RADIATING LIGHT.

2. *Physical Power.*
Sit comfortably and take five deep breaths.

Draw into you and around you the power of the sun. This exercise fully energises and balances the physical body. See a circle of crystal underneath your feet. Let your feet, your legs, your body, arms and head transform into clear quartz crystal. Focus into your spine, heart and head.

Take five deep breaths. Draw the power of the sun into you. Absorb sunlight into your physical body. See the energy being held in the body.

Take five deep breaths. Your physical power is increasing. YOUR BODY IS POWERFUL, VIBRANT AND HEALTHY.

3. *Being In The Heart.*

Sit comfortably and take five deep breaths. Close your eyes.

Visualise pale pink light that is your heart. Allow this delicate pale pink light to expand and become more powerful with each breath. The colour and power of the heart will become stronger and stronger, energising you in every part of your physical body.

Take five deep breaths. Connect with the power, peace and harmony of being in your heart. YOUR HEART IS POWERFUL.

4. *Who Am I?*

Take five deep breaths, sitting comfortably with your eyes gently closed.

Expand the heart and mind. Get a sense of how you feel. Just note this. As you explore how you feel, allow this to fall away. This falls away like an envelope around your physical body. As you reach deeper, you see or sense a body of powerful light that is really you. Really see it. Just for a moment allow yourself to take a glimpse of the power that is really you.

Take five deep breaths. Can you connect with it and expand it in the power of the sun? You may also connect with a colour or colours that represent the power of who you are. See yourself energise and expand. YOU ARE TRULY POWERFUL.

5. *I Am Power.*

Take five deep breaths, sitting comfortably with your eyes closed.

Expand brilliant sunlight through your heart and mind. Connect with love. Connect with the word power. How might you visualise how you can write POWER powerfully? What colour or colours might you use? See yourself writing power, in a powerful way. You may write slowly; be precise. You may write with exquisite beauty and consideration. See this as a slogan that you can wrap and wrap around yourself many times. Recognise: I AM POWER.

Take five deep breaths. Let the brilliance and comfort of what you have created emanate through your being.

6. Archangel Michael. Take five deep breaths. Centring self and expanding. Awaken your connection with archangel Michael. Use name or symbol. This exercise will transform deepest fear and powerfully awaken you to the truest sense of who you are. Awakening your divinity and power to begin to heal and awaken self. Michael is powerfully energising and transforming on all levels

CHAPTER 7

USING YOUR POWER EFFECTIVELY

"I grew up in southern Africa and loved my life, as any child does who is settled and happy. I loved Africa and although my family was quite poor, we still had a nice enough house and I enjoyed school, which was just across the road. My parents were strict and had to work really hard and long hours to keep our heads above water financially, but they also made sure that we did things as a family at the weekend, going into the hills for picnics or swimming or just window-shopping in town.

I was distraught when, one evening, they announced that we would be leaving Africa to go and live in England, where my father was from. I was eleven and I always knew it was a bad decision. I think that that is when things started to unravel a little around the edges for me.

Within just a few weeks of telling us we'd be leaving Africa, my father went to find work in England. It was several months before we left Africa with my mum to join him. They told us we could always come back to Africa if we didn't like it. My last memory of our home was seeing Elizabeth, the lady who had looked after my sister and I nearly all our young lives, running down the drive in tears, begging for us not to leave. I knew I would never see her again.

We arrived at Heathrow in the UK to green, green fields and huge lanes of motorways, we'd never seen anything like it! I thought that the fields must be irrigated constantly and that the Houses of Parliament were a grand palace. Suddenly, we were foreigners and even though we spoke the same language, every nuance and gesture held different meanings. I had had no idea that countries and people could be so different. As a result of moving, I became a different person, not just one of the crowd any more but a foreigner, and in those pre-teen years that's the last place you want to be. I think from this point, identity became a real issue for me.

All my family were sickeningly and desperately homesick and very lonely. We tried to pull together but we were all just too unhappy, my father was impossibly difficult and my mum couldn't handle it. She went back to Africa, first to sell our home, then a second time for a break.

But really my Mum couldn't bear life in England and so two years after arriving in England, she decided to divorce my father and go back to Africa for good. My sister and I wanted to go with her but in the end we stayed in England. The day my mum left, my sister and I were packed off to school for the day. Saying goodbye to my mum that morning broke my heart; I thought I would never see her again. I burrowed my head into my books and didn't come up for air again until I left, aged 18, to go to university. What a relief to leave that town, find pastures new and get a life, my own life!

Instead, I surrounded myself with friends who had very strong person-alities. I was also very uncommitted in any of my relationships; in fact I wasn't really ready for any kind of commitment to anyone. I had had to be so self-sufficient from my early teens and my parents' marriage had been so difficult, that I just didn't want to go there.

For several years I did a demanding but boring job in journalism, before swapping it for a job that was also demanding in PR. This time, though, I found myself totally out of my depth and in my late 20s, left that job to escape everything and to travel the world. It turned out to be a tough journey because the past, quite simply, caught up with me and I had to do a lot of grieving. I went back to Africa (big mistake) and then came back to England (bigger mistake), desperately homesick once again. It opened all the old wounds, I think, and it took me many months to climb out of a very severe depression for which I felt I could seek no help. I was angry, too – I couldn't believe that I was stuck in that same place! So what did I do? I buried myself in my work, once again, and focused on journalism and earning a living.

Eventually, thankfully, all those contracts started to slip by, one by one, and in my early thirties I was forced to start looking at what I really intended to do with myself for the rest of my life..."

Caroline

"**The year is 2003. As I began working, the focus of the life vision session was definition of self, partnership and her resistance was affecting Caroline's flow into future. The key was her heart and clear communication in all her relationships. What was particularly clear was using power more selectively and wisely so that she was in balance. The information defined a more versatile, dynamic Caroline in specific areas of work, healing, relationships and spirituality.**"

The session would re-direct her more positively than we realised. She was learning to develop greater resilience around others. In understanding others she was learning to develop spiritually. Taking control was key and developing greater confidence in self. The work would be on personality, ego and breaking free of any constraints on this level. A shift into healing self would also bring a consideration to have children in the future. This would develop her maternal instinct, her confidence issues, her connection and detachment with the world, work and her family.

The information I accessed brought qualities of definite presence, charisma, confidence and spiritual confidence. But because of her focus into spirituality there was a discrepancy of balance between work and her spiritual development. Her development as a healer would eventually contain the energy of her day-to-day work. In terms of career development and consolidation of work, the direction of work would take 3 streams: journalism in books and travel, negotiating contracts and pioneering projects in educational resources via the Internet. It is interesting to note that the session was in February 2003 and this internet project began in spring 2004 and was launched in Autumn 2005.

This direction of work would bring confidence, control and creative potential. Caroline would become advisor and creator in her work. I would assist her in recognising her power to realise her dreams.

Following are Caroline's comments on her readings.

"I think that my first soul purpose reading was a bit of a wake-up call and started me thinking more about where I was going; other than I wanted my work to be more creative. However, I wasn't actively trying to make anything happen, so it was kind of done for me. I had reached a point where I had lost my three major (but unfulfilling) contracts, along with quite a few friends, my home was in chaos - and my bank account t- and I was in an all time low both physically and inspirationally.

My main concern at that point was how drained I was feeling, and the reading gave me practical help by pointing out how I could build my energy - what I should be eating, drinking, and even the kind of exercise I should be doing, that I should be more grounded. It also pointed out that travel was important to me.

It was really important to get those things right, because until I felt up to scratch physically, I wouldn't have the energy to build my life around me. I really had to face the fact that it was up to me to get on with life.

The reading helped me to put my career in focus - I was dipping in and out of various freelance contracts that weren't really taking me anywhere. I needed to focus into one area, and the reading helped me to see it as publishing. Well, by then it had to be because I was about to lose the rest! Tracey also sensed that I should be doing more in terms of management, overseeing projects multi-media. I felt more able to take on something more challenging, so I started looking for different types of work and being open to change."

By April 2004 Caroline was developing an exciting, creative, informative multi-media project that would have huge implications on children's journalism and children's books. She started working to secure funding for the project.

Her career is now dynamic and fulfilling. She is excited about the development of her career and her project. The soul reading has brought energy and creativity to her life. She has also connected back into travelling and travelled to Egypt and Jordan.

"The session also suggested that I should be working more with people around me, than keeping myself tucked away in my own office. This was important because it helped me get my life moving again. I started working one day each week in a publishing-based office, which built my contracts, helped me focus on this area, and gave me a bit of inspiration for some new projects. It felt to me that I had committed to one area.

While I have had a few psychic readings over the years, and while they have often highlighted to me how important it is for me as a person to get my working life right, and that I should travel more, they never said why. I have also been told various things would happen (by other psychics - which often didn't), but they made me feel like life would happen to me, rather than I needed to go out and live it in my way. Now I feel like that I have the tools at my fingertips - things like writing, travel and my work projects - to enable me to use my energy creatively and to be a more active player in my life. And I think that's a really good thing to know!

Time and time again in my Life Purpose sessions with Tracey over the years, she said that I'd be working with children's books and helping develop educational tools for younger children. I was very much helped with the website in a reading I had with Tracey in the Spring 2005. This confirmed I was on the right track (finally!) and she gave me very practical, very precise information about how the website would be struc- tured and how it would develop. Knowing what you need to do is one thing, but having this kind of detailed information during a reading is invaluable.

Another thing Tracey always said in the Soul Purpose readings was that my emotional life / relationships wouldn't be sorted out until I got my working life right. Well, she was right again. Soon after I'd put in my application for funding for my website, I went on holiday to Jordan and met this gorgeous guy. Tracey had emailed me just before I left: 'There's a man coming into your life' and she was right – even so it took me totally by surprise. Best of all, on the day we finally got together, I received confirmation of funding for my website! It seems that work and play do go hand in hand for me.

It is now the end of 2005 and I am totally confident that I am now living my life purpose and that I am going in the right direction. The only problem I have now is how to fit in all the things I feel I want to do! My working life has transformed. I am completely engaged in my project to set up a children's book's website and am networking like crazy to get it the support it should have among educators, book based organisations and the government.

Once I committed to the project 18 months ago (and got on with what I was meant to be doing in terms of life purpose!), it almost took on a life of its own and it's been a creative, fulfilling experience to get it up and running. I feel like I am working with very different energies now, as I have to be very precise, organised and detailed as well as visionary to make the project succeed.

I am also aiming to set up a charitable side of the business, both to help people in the educational field in the Western world, but also to help fund educating children in developing countries, I am certain that I need to do this, too and that I will get the help I need to do so.

I have to be a different person from the one I was four or five years ago to make all this succeed. I no longer sit and wait for things to happen. I have to be confident, open to any new ideas, and driven, so finding my life purpose has changed me. I don't have the same fears and depression that I used to get – even if I do get anxious, I know how to deal with it now. I am also pulling on other strengths that I haven't used before, such as people management and motivation.

My life structure feels much more open, too. I am planning to move house to live with my boyfriend and I want my home environment to be very different from where I live now. I can already see the kind of house I want to live in, and where, and I'm totally confident that I will get there in the next few months.

My relationship with my family has changed as well. We have always been a very close family but now I also feel that my parents see me as an independent person. I know they are pleased about where I am going in life.

As well as working hard, I want to have time for the things that make me tick and make this world a fun place to be, especially travel, and I am determined that along the way I will set up a project for the environment – that's another goal I now feel I am capable of fulfilling. In all, I really feel like I am going somewhere now, rather than just drifting, and it's a good place to be!"

Caroline's case study outlines the possibilities that occur when you begin to access the powerful psychological and inspirational alchemy of life vision. Perhaps for all of us it is a time to assess our lives. If you are feeling static within your life vision, Caroline's case study encourages you to take steps into self-discovery and into a life vision that is vibrant, alive and creative.

What happens when you feel stuck? Many of us, close down, detach from living or barely survive or we can face a powerful realisation that life vision is not being developed to potential. It takes great courage to admit failure in friendships that don't provide support. It takes courage to face fears of a loving relationship. It takes courage to really create and live our dreams.

The question arises how do you connect into a potential life vision blueprint that allows you to flow in dynamic new directions into new experiences beyond limitations? Powerful life vision encourages you to strive to discover an ever-expansive life vision blue print that expands with an ever-expanding world and universal vision. Life vision moves constantly beyond what we have come to know.

Some of you experiencing the Awakening will be experiencing difficult periods of intense self-realisation and life transformation. This can make you feel unbalanced, tired, restless, directionless and confused. Others will already be conscious, awake, alive and vibrant in soul vision. Every experience is valid- to dissolve the old and harness new consciousness. This period will last until you have moved fully into new perception of who you are and recognition of what you can contribute to new world vision. Accessing your life purpose is vital- then you can respond by recognising and creating perfectly with each significant person, place and activity to activate your dynamic life and world vision.

Life Vision Affirmations

- I am loved

- I am inspirational and creative

- I am a healer in my work and creator

- I am powerful in my life

Make Your Own Life Vision Programme

Write down what you feel or think YOUR POWER is to you. It may be a word. An image. A place. Examples: HEALTH, VIBRANCY, ENERGY, VISION, CLARITY, LOVE.

1. *Power.*

Sit comfortably and close your eyes.

Take five deep breaths. Sense or imagine your body turn into liquid gold. Feel the power and peace in your body. How centred you can become by focussing on your breath and vision/feeling. As you connect with this, where do you feel your power centre? In the heart or the head? Focus and expand these areas in two deep breaths.

I AM POWERFUL. Visualise your body filled with gold.

2. *Being In Your Light.*

Sit comfortably and close your eyes.

Take five deep breaths. Imagine a diamond of light from the centre of your chest. Visualise it clearly. Expand your diamond light from this area so that it is surrounding you. This exercise develops heart power and heart confidence. The strength to communicate who you really are.

3. *Power Qualities.*

Write down a list of qualities that you wish to bring to you and your life. Start with your personal life. For example: love.

Sit comfortably and close your eyes. Visualise an image of love or sense the depth of how love can be. Feel it or see it in your heart centre. You can equally visualise the word 'love' as a slogan metres and metres long that you can wrap around yourself. You feel it expanding through you and into and from your heart centre. Examples: FOCUS, INTEGRITY, BALANCE, CREATIVITY, PEACE, JOY

4. *Relationships.*

Write down the power qualities you would like to create in your relationships. What do you look for in another person? Take one quality at a time and visualise an image of that particular quality. For example: honesty.

Take five deep breaths. Sit comfortably with eyes closed.

Visualise or sense what it feels like to be open to honesty of self or from others. See and sense how you flow with this quality. You can expand and allow your imagery to flow. Examples: COURAGE, OPENESS, INSIGHT, GENTLENESS

5. *Love.*

Write down the qualities you would like to create in a partnership. You can equally draw how you would like the relationship to be. Choose one quality.

Sit comfortably with your eyes closed. Connect with the power of your heart centre. Connect with your diamond of light.

Take five deep breaths. Connect with a knowing or feeling of love. Expand your heart centre. Open to your power to create feeling and knowing these qualities are within. Expand your heart and let this quality flow through you and outside of yourself. Into partnership. Into future partnership. Examples: LOVE, TRUTH, SUPPORT, BALANCE, HARMONY, CREATIVITY, FREEDOM

6. Connect with Gabriel. Awakening self-love and the perfection of who you truly are. Gabriel awakens the creator- allowing you to truly explore and create authentic self into the world- empowered.

CHAPTER 8

INTEGRATING YOUR SENSITIVITY

"1964: I was born, a middle child, in Cornwall, to working class parents. On my Mother's side was mental illness – on my Father's side addictions.

1967: I had a traumatic experience in which I partly left my body. I was very ungrounded.

1968: I decided to become a teacher. Childhood was isolated, lonely, unhappy, desperate.

1982-1986: I went to College. Finally I was with like-minded people.

The end of 1987- 1992: I taught primary children in Cornwall. A relationship I was in broke up so I moved back to my parents. There I was confronted with my Father's alcoholism.

1992-1994: Worked with severely emotionally deprived children (9-16 year old boys) in a therapeutic community. Hard work - 70 hours a week, 6 days a week - continued my inner journey through therapy. Therapist died of cancer on my twenty ninth birthday. Very difficult time. I shut myself away from life and concentrated on work.

Working in the community I learnt such a huge amount about myself and others.

1994-1995: Lived in Cornwall and had a complete rest. I went to Skyros and to India for two months. The India trip was great. I travelled round different ashrams with two followers of Osho.

1995-1997: Worked in Cambodia doing development work. I trained trainers and they trained primary school teachers. During the last year I managed the office and was in charge of 40 staff. A fantastic experience. I loved it. I went on holiday to Australia and stayed at Ken and Elizabeth Mellors mediation centre and I went to Pune in India to Osho's ashram where I took Sannyas and changed my name to Veet Chaya (beyond shadow).

1998-2000. I went back to England to work at the Osho school in

Devon. Fantastic experience. The motto was 'the chance of a lifetime' and it was for the kids and the staff. The ethos was upon trusting the kids' intelligence. I had to drop all I believed about teaching and all I believed about students. At Ko Hsuan school I learned to dance on a shifting carpet!

I loved working as a team towards a common vision with like-minded people. For part of my time there I shared the role of head teacher. During this time I worked weekly with a mystic - watching my emotional reactions to events and people.

2000-2001: I lived in Somerset with a family and taught their child who had ADHD.

2001-Now: moved to London due to a new relationship. I work for Brent tuition service. I tutor children who are out of school, excluded, sick, moved house and have no school place. Resumed therapy as I did a foundation year in Integrative Arts Psychotherapy. Three years later, the course is long finished but the therapy continues. But hopefully not for much longer.

Relationship finished, I have gained strength since.

All the things that I have done in my life have been about my own healing journey. I have spent the first half of my life trying to make sense of what happened when I was three. I also did not want to go mad, which is what happened to my granddad, aunt and grandmother. At that time I shut down my sensitivity as I felt it was like a handicap."

Joanne

Joanne came to see me in June 2005. This session and the subsequent work Joanne has achieved in The Awakening System has really demonstrated that she has a truly inspiring of sensitivity. It is now 2007 and Joanne is awakening to her empowered purpose as channel and sensitive.

"You have a foundation of analysis which prevents you from being grounded. This is about the next stages - where to go next - very

gently. There are even questions over home. This is a primary factor as you need to put your roots down. "I need nature"- having a garden, working with plants. This is about what you place around yourself in a very permanent way. Putting your roots down is very important – you need a home for you. Surround yourself in colour. It is not your sensitivity - it is the way you can slide into a more comfortable lifestyle. The right move. The right transition. The right property. Peace and security. This is exactly what you need, emotionally and mentally. You seem to restrict yourself mentally. On one level, there is such a need to stop thinking so much and you have to say 'I do deserve'. You then have the foundations to be very dynamic and very successful. There is a lot of independence. "Lets create a new me." One that is very colourful, very solid, very precise in terms of the way that you use your energy and who you attract. Clarity, precision and perfection around you - especially the home.

There is still a link into London - Home Counties. A rural feel. There is also getting the home right and to belong to community. This is giving you the support so that your sensitivity can be turned around. People who are environmentally aware and nature aware. This is a special interest of yours.

A huge decision to really let emotional baggage go and with your next move - that's just it. A long drawn emotional journey. These are the last drops. You are in exactly the right position now. All your spirituality is resting now in the physical. It's starting to become valid in the way you need to be and where you need to be. This will make you open doors in the way that you consider yourself as a healer. This is particularly important as there is a side to you that wants to do conventional healing work. I certainly have a link to how you can work more as a communicator as well in healing. Working with listening - counselling and spirituality. You have been looking so much for your niche - to govern your sensitivity better. The only way to govern it is to work with it, exhaust it. You need to stretch yourself.

Getting the right location for home is important with this, too.

You have been gathering a lot of strength and coming back into your own. You have had problems with partnership. This has taught you about your own power. The partner has brought you to where you are but has also held you back. Long drawn and painful relationship. You being in the position of parenting and this not being sufficient for you. The dynamic of what is left is freedom. You need your independence and own space. We need to bring in more self approval. Your mother was a great communicator, quite forceful. You need to take the right qualities for yourself. Everything about you is about to take a new chapter - home, work- you need to work with people. There is so much energy to develop professionally in healing work. Professional counselling dynamics- more interactive and intuitive. Intuitive counselling. You need to engage in creativity as a meditative tool. Mediation doesn't work as well as being creative. Nature, trees, water as well. In relationships- friendships can be an illusion. You want these to be genuine. You are very tired of this. A real sense of knowing that you need to support yourself from your goddess energy. You have had a lot of conflict in your feminine energy. You come into a much more confident woman in 36 months. You need a partner who is a healer. You need to be connected to London."

"I considered the West Country but it didn't feel right."

"Your next relationship will teach you about romantic love. You need Englishness. Pretty countryside. This honours the opposites with in you. Culture and the arts in London as well. You need to do psychic training. Because you are more spiritually aware you can turn the concept of who I am on its head. It's about how much you can draw to yourself and you are not used to it. Your gifts- creatively and communicatively can come to life. Karma and life have left you drained and exhausted. Child comes into this- linked into nature and interlinked to the correct partnership. Use who you are to teach this child. You are coming into your true contracts. Work with your intuition. The way that the physical is mirroring exactly who you are. Getting everything in the right place. Everything will fall into place. A real turning point to really come into your own power and never go back to what you once were. I don't see you being trampled ever again. Administer who you are in life. You need the anchoring.

Work. Make a decision by the end of the year in terms of what you want to do next. Train and work part time. Develop your creativity. You've never been in the right place to live. You have worked very hard - your mental , emotional and spiritual but not the material level. The work you will do will be very soul orientated. Do not doubt yourself. Creative and spiritual. Settle into who you are and the place you live. You need to work with your intelligence- intuitive psychology. Your eccentricity needs to come through. Its great! You are a clear communicator."

Joanne's comments

"I have realised that I am a very sensitive person and in fact should be working with it in some way. I hope that by clearing my own emotional difficulties I will be able to help others in some way.

I came to Tracey's classes as I had already done a year's foundation in psychic development and I was looking for a new teacher who could support the next stage of my development. I was inspired by Tracey as she' walks her talk'. She has shown me that my sensitivity is empowering!

I have been through a huge crisis - physically, emotionally and mentally. Before it started I had a reading in which Tracey looked at all aspects of my life. It was a fantastic reading and I really felt that she got to grips with my essence. Through the reading I have been encouraged to follow my intuition and guidance and to trust life.

I am not well 100% but am getting better all the time. I feel as though I have been through a huge transformational experience and am now prepared to take full responsibility for who I am and what I am meant to do on the planet.

I am not yet in life purpose but feel very sure that I soon will be. Tracey is teaching me how to control my own energy and I am beginning to monitor myself much more as to what I need. I can see all the emotional healing that I have done and am still completing has been necessary. But once complete my future will no longer be controlled by my past. I want to continue to work with Tracey so that I can refine my skills but also so that I can continue to be inspired and step into who I am.

I want to help other people to turn their lives around. I would like to work with the emotions, psychically and spiritually. Through working with Tracey I feel as though anything and everything is possible. That I am the creator of my life and that I can manifest what I want. Also that in this life healing is truly possible and that debts from past lives can be cleared leaving one free to really live from one's true essence, in this moment.

I feel that Tracey has offered me a fantastic gift and I am very grateful."

Joanne has opened a wonderful gift in exploring her psychic and intuitive abilities. It has been a pleasure to watch such a gentle and powerfully sensitive soul come to life. Every week allows her to gather her strength and focus. In weeks that Joanne may feel out of flow, her developing gift as a channel brings her strength and courage. She has an amazing journey ahead of her. Her intelligence brings a depth to the work she brings to others.

When I worked with Joanne, in her life vision session, we tapped into her potential as a powerful and dynamic intuitive psychologist. This is exactly what has come to life in the work she does which is so healing. Joanne becomes the powerful communicator and healer that she knows she is and knows she can be. She comes to life. She is vibrant, happy and giving to everyone she works with. There is a wonderful spirituality in the work. The difference is that she really acknowledges her power and how alive her power can be through this work. Joanne will be a wonderful healer and powerful psychic. She will finally create a powerful life vision that fully acknowledges the pain of her past.

Life Vision Affirmations

- My sensitivity is powerful

- I am a powerful communicator

- I can create who I know I am

Life Power Programme

1. Power Of Spirituality.

Sit comfortably and close your eyes. Let the mind still and your heart feel powerful.

Take five deep breaths. Let your soul step forward. This is who you really are. Let the power of your soul or spirit emerge in your physical body. Through your mind and heart.

Take five deep breaths. Can you connect with an image that represents your spirituality? This may be a star, a religious or mystical symbol. Equally, modern spirituality can take on a symbol for peace or harmony. Expand your image. Allow that image to flow powerfully through your body.

Take five deep breaths. Surround yourself with radiant light. See your image being energised and empowered. Let yourself shine. Take five deep breaths.

2. Balancing.

Sit comfortably and close your eyes. Draw in the power of the sun. Let the light fill your mind. Let the light fill your heart. See and sense very bright white light above the head and allow it into your body. Focus on energising the heart. Bringing freedom to your emotions. Explore a sense of peace, clarity and well-being. Let these qualities flow beautifully through your being. Press your feet into the floor and anchor this inner power.

3. The Beauty Within.

Sit comfortably and close your eyes. Draw in the power of sunlight. Let the light fill your heart and mind. Connect with a sense of the power of your spirituality. You may use a symbol. Energise this symbol in the light that surrounds you. Press your feet into the floor.

Take five deep breaths. See the beauty that is within. Visualise who you really are. Step into the positive power and beauty of who you can truly be. You may visualise the most exquisite pearl. You may visualise the most beautiful sky or delicate butterfly. Let the delight of your imagination guide you. Let this image expand and energise you. YOUR INNER BEAUTY SHINES. Press your feet into the floor.

4. Holding That Beauty.

Sit comfortably and close your eyes. That superb image that defines your beauty within, allow it to shine through your entire being. Visualise it as strong even if it is the most delicate image imaginable. Surround it with golden light. See it vibrantly supported and stronger than ever.

Take five deep breaths and repeat visualising your image and surrounding it with golden light. Feel that you are truly strong and supported by who you truly are. YOU ARE POWERFUL.

5. Staying In Your Heart.

Sit comfortably with your eyes closed. Press your feet into the floor.

Energise your body in light. Surround yourself in solid, energising light. Focus into your heart power. Focus into the beauty of your heart power.

Take five deep breaths. See your heart energy flow. Recognise when you need to nurture the energy and power of the heart. See your heart powerfully and continuously energised. You have much strength. See yourself in modern life. See your heart centre powerfully and continuously energised whatever the situation. YOU ARE POWERFUL.

6. Connect with archangel Uriel. Archangel Uriel powerfully de-sensitises and transforms limiting emotional and psychic sensitivity whilst anchoring you into the world. Uriel awakens intelligent perspective and empowered psychological perspective. Whilst honouring the truest sense of spirituality and how that can be expanded into the modern world- Uriel is key as the alchemist in transforming self and your world.

CHAPTER 9

CONNECTING MIND AND BODY

"As a child I felt lonely and alienated. While an academically high achiever from very early, I perceived that something was not right. Whilst drawn to religion I found teachings I was receiving somewhat empty so I cut myself off from the Roman Catholic environment at the age of twelve. An anguished teenager I distinctively knew that "I did not Know"- though I didn't know what I didn't know.

I had low self esteem and felt different t- developed depression at around sixteen, which was to last for the next thirty years, only becoming more acute after my daughter was born twenty years ago. My depression was unrecognized by my environment or myself. I struggled with life, my daughter becoming the focus of my life. My marriage broke when my daughter was six. Very quickly I came to realize the wider reasons for existence. I followed personal development - in areas of self-hypnosis, mind techniques, past lives, karma and psychology. It lessened the burden of my existence but did not give me focus- I still felt I was a ship without a rudder- not knowing what to do in professional terms; not knowing and perhaps being afraid to find out what I really wanted to do. It feels now that most of my life has been a healing crisis- struggling, suffering from anxiety.

My first ever reading at The College of Psychic Studies in 1996 eased that. When the sensitive said, "You cleared so much in your life in the last six years on your own" I felt I was doing something right at last. Even so, after this I struggled on - with a feeling that my life was just skimming over what was important to me. I studied psychology and holistic therapies for reasons not entirely clear to me at the time. I was kind of pushed in this direction- or rather I pushed myself in this direction not exactly knowing why."

Tracey's first Life Vision session in 2003, had a very grounding effect on me - I saw that what I had studied helped me understand others better, that my life experiences made me much less judgemental and accepting of others. I found it difficult to accept that my path is of a healer and so sabotaged myself on the action that would hasten my development. The seed was planted though and things started to make sense. I recognised more peace in my life and a sense of belonging after all those years. I have been stubborn- I did not act until after my second session with Tracey - even though opportunities were landing in my lap.

I had a session with Tracey in 2005. I am now very clear about what I want from my future and full of hope that the opportunities I am presented with- I will take advantage of. I know now I deserve and I am capable. My purpose is to heal others- and by doing so heal myself and my relationships. Also, in this life it is important for me to be grounded firmly and embrace as my aspects of life on this planet as I can. I want to develop abundance consciousness- in terms of happiness, health, relationships and material things. I am learning to lead an independent life and be responsible for all aspects of my life - emotional, spiritual and material. I feel already blessed for my relationship with my daughter, my fellow traveller, without whom so many that helped me in my development would simply not happen. I am learning that there is a wall separating me from something - it is mainly built by me and that it is up to me to find the door. Working with Tracey has made it so much easier."

Maria

Session in June 2003

"Where is your mind-body connection? This is not about working on the body then working in the head. This connection needs to become more fluid for you. Your work is healing work; this is your purpose. I have a really strong sense of you being able to fuse the mind and the body work together. Rather than being a purist, you need to work with the body and mental level together. You are very good at body

memory work - going into your own body memories; the way that you feel issues very strongly in your body.

You have had to spend a lot of time going into very difficult energies and issues so the way that you need to work is through bodywork - releasing that in other people. You are so conscious of the way your body has been very dense and inflexible and you can work with people in that capacity through reflexology and massage. You have a lot of ability to intuit.

It feels like the psychology aspect is a very long journey for you. You have had to learn how to process for your self and trust your intuition so that it is finite. The psychology has made you strong- given you a sense of yourself- and this has been building so that you can come into your power as a healer. You are a healer. You are not only a mental level healer. You need to work with higher energies. You need to be in flow with meditation. You are very much a light worker. You find it very difficult to work with dense energies. Your vibration is very light- you attract people who need healing. Until you come into your authentic healing work- you are doing a lot of supporting work with friends and strangers. I feel you can be over supportive at times. You get tired very easily.

Archangel Uriel makes you aware of your psychic sensitivity and emotional sensitivity- you are very susceptible to feeling atmospheres in places and moods in people. You feel everything in your heart and solar plexus. As a child- you were not given the chance to make your own decisions- this is still coming through to you as an adult. Link into archangel Uriel and Michael- this will empower you. You have worries about being isolated from childhood.

But as an adult you don't have people around you who are isolating you. As a child- your mother was very fearful and depressed. It is part of your life purpose to support. You are very key in your family to change the patterns. You are the transformer. The same as you do a lot of transforming work with your friends. You need to focus upon energy work- this will allow you to flow from your soul energy. You are using and developing your intuition. You are proficient in psychology. This inner child- this uncertainty, this inability to make decisions is being transformed. It is interesting that your life purpose is half of your life is learning about not having control and then coming into your power in the second half. You are learning this through healing work- learning how to negotiate more control, to negotiate more with people. You have to be a healer in order for you to come into your own power.

Almost at times reflecting back what others are projecting onto you. The psychology work is particularly important for you in terms of your own sensitive and psychic protection. You need to do deep tissue massage work."

"I have just finished training."

"You need to pioneer techniques - fusing different ideas together."

"I have no confidence."

"Work with massage, reflexology and counselling sessions. This will bring rapid healing. You need to be practical. The learning is coming to an end. The financial concerns will force you into being the healer. Its bringing you into a very balanced way of working- the massage and counselling. You need to work on your physical energy through physical exercise- this would help you to resonate at the right level for you to express your life purpose powerfully.

Sometimes the physical body can't house this energy. You have a sluggish digestive system. You power issues lie more in the physical now. You have transcended many of your healing issues.

Now you have to start strengthening through physical exercise, diet and more water. You will start to de-sensitive in your every day life. To become contained and focussed. The bodywork will encourage control over your sensitivity by placing you in contact with people. The psychology will give you the respect you crave. This will bring you emotional balance. You need to do healing work to show your child balance because the child is showing tendencies of being sensitive as well. Showing you how to change your energy as well. Archangel Michael can also help your child as this archangel brings in a sense of protection. Your child is an indigo and is very psychic. She is very creative - needing to paint. Her artistic side is very strong."

"She is going to art college."

"She is also teaching you how you need to recognise your own beauty and confidence in your femininity."

Session in November 2005:

"You are more focussed on your healing work in different ways. It is important that you push yourself forward. How you package and present yourself- so that you can market you and your work more. You need to push your work in a more professional way- you need to be considering new places to work from. You are looking at developing healing techniques and tailoring clients needs. A fusion of techniques- your work is complimentary and unique to the individual. You work with healing stress. You need to market yourself in stress, relaxation, streamlining busy lifestyle, stress management, talking with your clients- a therapeutic angle.

The more you practice and market yourself - the more you will work with professionals. Stress management, physical tension, understanding, relaxing, calming, dissolving tension, physical fatigue - to be placed in a leaflet. You are working with Shiatsu and reflexology in a corporate environment - a whole package for management and groups of workers. You are an expert and professional stress management consultant. You have so may different tools. Look at ways to take it away from just massage, list different techniques. List what you can target in your clients- stress, fatigue, unwinding stress, relaxation. You can offer a bespoke programme to executives. You are not defining yourself as a healer. You are recommending packages and contracts of several months with professional, corporate businesses, banking and finance.

You are targeting offices by making yourself mobile. You feel very focussed. Let it happen. Start creating. The work is also being given by a teacher connected with you. He will franchise work out to you. You need to ask for it He has connections with the city. Start to guide yourself in the right directions. You need to ask for this!"

There was confirmation of this from Maria - her Shiatsu teacher had offered her work in the city.

"You are overhauling your work. Your balance of energy will be better. At home- you can read and develop spiritually. There is also a tendency to stay connected with your clients in your healing sessions. Completely disconnect from these healing sessions so that you come back to your authentic self. The important thing to do is to recharge and replenish. This will maximise your energy field. You will have resilience and strength particularly in a corporate environment. More centred and balanced.

This lifetime concerns how you work emotionally and spiritually. Make sure that your sanctuary is home - is solid. You want to be more spiritual with more meditation and the ancient. Clear types of meditation - chanting, yogic breath work, ancient techniques in contrast with your corporate work. Being and honouring how gentle you are. Next year is about working hard on a spiritual level for you."

Maria's is another powerful case study and inspiration for us all in our journeys of self-discovery and healing. A lifetime of emotional healing and journey into self and her power had led Maria in many directions-psychology, her relationships and healing. Most powerful of all, the realisation that indeed she could not flow until she had finally accepted who she was and her life vision. As Maria's grasp and confidence of her life vision grew, her deep, innate spiritual nature expanded into her life in the most practical way. Her life vision and her life experiences were vital in evolving into a sensitive and empowered healer. Her power within became a true source of inspiration, healing and living. She could finally come into a place of freedom- releasing her from the past to emanate confidence so that she could truly create her life.

Life Vision Affirmations

- I am empowerment

- I am freer than ever before

- I am being, I am creating

Life Vision Programme

1. *I Am Power.*

Take five deep breaths, sit comfortably with your eyes closed. Connect with what power means to you.

Take five deep breaths. What symbol represents your power? You may see yourself with the power to heal self. You may see yourself with the power to be happy. Connect with that image or symbol. Let it expand. Let it energise you.

Take five deep breaths. I AM POWER. Press your feet into the floor.

2. *Life Power*.

Think about writing down positive life qualities you need to create in your life. They may be qualities of courage, freedom, peace, harmony. What do you feel you would like to really anchor into your life first?

Take five deep breaths. Close your eyes and sit comfortably. Let the mind expand. Let the heart expand. You are exquisite power and love. Which quality do you feel you need most? Gently connect with it.

Take five deep breaths. Expand how that quality may positively feel. Can you visualise how you might be empowered in that particular quality? Let it shine through you and flow.

Take five deep breaths. I AM POWERFUL. I AM SUPPORTED.

3. *Powerful Work Vision*.

This exercise will help you create and define your work vision based on your modern spirituality. This exercise will support you even if the work you do is not perfect.

Close your eyes and sit comfortably.

Take five deep breaths. Bring to mind work or future work. Energise your heart and mind in the power of the sun. See yourself surrounded in this power. Now access a more powerful work vision. Connect with a sense of what you would like to bring to life at work. It may be harmony. It may be confidence to honour oneself with a pay rise. It may be to connect with the work that you have longed for.

Take five deep breaths once again. Connect with sunlight in and around you. Open your heart and mind. Connect with your positive work vision that empowers you. YOU HAVE THE POWER TO CREATE.

4. *Living Your Power*.

Write down the qualities of how you wish to live your life. Select one to work with. Visualise what this is. Visualise how this may take shape in your life.

Take five deep breaths. POWER QUALITY: CENTEREDNESS. How

can this quality manifest in your life? Where in your life do you wish to develop centeredness? Visualise or feel what centeredness could be. And expand this.

Take five deep breaths. Where could you bring this to your life. For example: work, relationships, modern life. See yourself bringing this centeredness to an area of your life. Examples: PEACE, INSPIRATION, ENERGY, HOPE, CONFIDENCE

5. *Healing.*

Let your heart and mind expand. Take five deep breaths.

Sense and visualise your physical body. Your heart and your mind.

Take five deep breaths. Energise in powerful light. See your body. Feel your body. Connect with crystal in your feet, your legs, your body, your arms and hands. Focus upon the clearest crystal in your brain and spine. Energise in light.

Take five deep breaths. YOUR POWER IS TO HEAL SELF.

6. Connect with archangel Uriel as name or symbol. Uriel will awaken expansion into new energy levels and insight into authentic self. With archangel Uriel- even your physical energy levels will be expanded. Your mind and heart energised and focussed. Uriel brings deepest empowerment and sense of your divine and personal power- thus anchoring self into the world- centring and anchoring you into your life. Your sensitivity and spirituality is empowered for modern world living.

CHAPTER 10

COMMUNICATING ON A NEW LEVEL

"I came to London from Athens (Greece) in 1993 to study Art & Design. After my trials and tribulations with the art world, I decided to change direction and study a business degree combined with European languages. I was quite confused in those days about my direction in life and none of it kept me really satisfied – I remember studying just for the sake of doing it rather than anything else.

In my last year at university, I found myself quite stressed and disappointed with my close relationships – romantic and friendships and I embarked on a journey of self-healing, initially reading self-help books, working with shamanic journeying etc. It was through the shamanic work that I found my first healing teacher. I saw a leaflet, I went to his workshop and I found myself immediately hooked! It seemed that whatever this person was talking about be it life, energies, healing, unseen worlds made so much sense. I wanted more of it! I continued doing workshops with the same teacher including a practitioners intensive.

From there, more exploration into healing work followed. I was enjoying every minute of it but found myself somehow questioning my direction (again) and not knowing whether this is what I was meant to be doing in life. And if yes, what type of healing work would be appropriate for me? It was then that I found Tracey. At first I visited her for a consultation. She confirmed my instincts that healing work was what I was meant to be doing and I found her fascinating, really inspiring. Tracey invited me to work with her and attend her classes in psychic development. I didn't take up that invitation until a couple of years after as I didn't think at the time that I had any sort of ability to do psychic work.

Through practising healing, I found myself accessing a variety of information about my clients' emotional states, past and present. The more I did it the more accurate I seemed to become. I got intrigued. I

*wanted to explore and stretch these new-found abilities more. I remem-
bered Tracey and her invitation and I decided to do a beginners
workshop. Tracey is a fantastic teacher. She demystified psychic work and
presented all aspects of the workshop in a clear and straightforward way
that enabled us to feel empowered and competent even as beginners. I
continued working with Tracey and still do to the present day.*

*The system that Tracey presents has made a real difference in my life.
It has progressively redefined my idea of who I really am and continues
to do so the more I work with it. It has given me the opportunity to explore
and connect with skills and abilities that I never knew I had and reuse
some others in a new, dynamic and more confident way. It has enabled me
to become more focused about what I really want to do with my life and
approach it creatively by working with my unique characteristics and
engaging me to stretch them to their maximum potential through ongoing
work. The more my understanding of the Awakening System deepens the
more I see its creative potential and its value as a means to live life in a
happier, more dynamic and fulfilling way.*

*The Awakening System differs considerably from any other work I
have done before, for it is a very empowering system that allows you to
determine and explore who you really are and thus heal yourself and your
issues by remaining focused on your power and truth while touching upon
sensitive areas. It is multi-faceted and can be used to channel information
on anything one wishes to focus on whether it is themselves or another
person etc. It gives a great discipline and solid foundation for any sort of
psychic/healing work.*

*Working with Tracey and the Awakening System has taught me the
value of being grounded and present every moment of my day and how to
do it. It has considerably improved my quality of life, my work and
relationships in specific by enabling me to redefine my boundaries and
find patience and a sense of direction. My own healing journey is a
combination of all the above. It is an ongoing journey!*

As to my life purpose – I think now I am more in it than I have ever been."

Anguela

Session 2003

"You are very stuck mentally. No matter which way you go you can't resolve relationship. This is closing your heart centre. You are both questioning the relationship. You can't connect. You are entering a massive change. The gap between you is getting bigger. You are not connecting. Communication is the issue. You are spending less time with him. He makes you solid. He can be quite soothing for you. You are moving into a very fast period and his energy is too slow. You are ready to open up to the next chapter. More visual, more travel. You have total commitment- when you commit in marriage. You have to be clear especially with other people around you. You are changing - there is so much change. To be free. You can be very daring.

Your partner is very home-based. He counts on you as being life-long partner. You are moving into a period where you travel and meet a lot of people from other countries. You have a passion for life as much as you have a passion for relationship. You are torn. You need to be stronger over who influences you. You have such conflict around security and being free. All of his focus is on you. You fit together very well. You need to be let free. He is making this difficult for you - he fears this is the end of the relationship. This is incorrect. He has other relationships where he has been rejected so he expects this.

Expectations are key - part of you is so daring. It is very possible that you stay together. You also have a lot of respect for your relationship. You are serious; re-thinking."

"I am changing and he isn't."

But a lot of the people you have around you are not grounded - you are very susceptible. This is very difficult for you. You are surrounded by a lot of people who are not taking responsibility. You are drawn to another person but this is more about what you can offer as a healer to him. This is not partnership. We go back to your partner. You need to be clearer about your own issues. You need to be adored by people. You need to be clear with your energy - your boundaries. Your partner is mature. He is completely different to the people you have around you. Pull the relationship back on track - be more philosophical, less serious. A lot of your focus needs to be harnessed in self. You are working creatively and intellectually. You make people matter as much as your partner. Get priorities right. He can really nurture you."

"But he doesn't talk to me."

"You can make this work on a very deep level. If you were more grounded then you would have a level of protection - you are very susceptible to what other people want you to do. Part of you is waiting. You need to be stimulated intellectually - study. You need to occupy your mind continuously. Part of your pathway is to develop intellectually - your partner complements this. You have a lot of friends who are not focussed. You need to be around much more focussed people. Partner is stabilising. You are desperate to be inspired.

You are not sure where you need to be based - where you live with partnership. Life is so different outside of your home. You are living two lives. You have such a potential to be academic - in healing. It's not about doing healing for the sake of doing healing, or yoga for the sake of doing yoga. You have two choices to be free but you will never be a good healer if you are not grounded. You are being given this choice. Your partner does not take anything from you at all which is a relief. You are doing so much healing work that you do not have any energy left for your relationship. Look at how your energy relates to people. You need to be clear. If you become very serious about your pathway- then the relationship will work. He does see you as the future mother of his children. You need to be more grounded about your purpose. This is now playtime. You need to become serious. You need to focus your energy.

You have a lot of creativity.

You are not grounded and this can lead you to get hurt. Your partner is always there for you - sincerity. The people you have had around you have been taking you further and further away from your relationship. You are healing all of these people. Your purpose is healer. You are really afraid of being on your own. Do not take the pathway that is only healing- independent and on your own. Or you have the choice of being stabilised and supported by your partner. You don't want to be on your own."

"I don't want to spend my life alone."

"Your intellect has to be focussed into healing techniques. Travel to America. You both need to travel together- this will bring you close together- so close. This is also about how you feel you can get closer to him. This will help the relationship flower. He is your companion- your soul mate on a deep, deep level. You feel lost if you are not around him. He sees you for what you are."

Anguela is an adult indigo. An indigo is "one who displays a new or unusual set of psychological attributes and shows a pattern of behaviour generally undocumented before."- The Indigo Children, Lee Carol and Jan Tober. I work with many adult indigos who at this time of awakening (2007 to 2025) are powerfully activating life purpose and awakening to empowered sensitivity and world vision. For the older indigos- the decades of acute sensitivity, healing, knowing and finding purpose are over. For so many of the older indigos- the feelings of isolation, disconnection and dis-empowerment has been so common but never losing sight for one second- authenticity. Feeling mis-understood and not fitting has been key. It is only now that the importance of authenticity and expanding life purpose and life vision is key. It is now important for all of us- especially indigos to awaken and truly create a new world vision. In honouring life purpose, you honour and create an authentic world vision.

Indigos have a deep authenticity or spirituality perspective no matter what. Perhaps the difficulty of their journey in the old world vision was to truly hold and honour who they are. Live it and be it- whilst so many others were still sleeping. At times incredibly difficult in a me! me! me! era. Perhaps the beauty of their journey is to heal and understand self and others. Perhaps their journey has been one of waiting- for exactly the right conditions to awaken as we move out of the old world vision. As we move into new world vision, indigos are being powerfully awakened and empowered to inspire and create change no matter who or what is limiting. At last, vital authenticity for self and the world- indigos playing a vital role in the way humanity creates a new world vision. The new world vision is authenticity- this is where the role of indigos is key! As we enter meltdown into authenticity- the indigos will hold new world vision in empowered sensitivity. In a consciousness that reflects conscious healing and conscious creation of the world. It is the beginning of awakening and a new consciousness for humanity. It is worth noting here that indigos are present in all generations.

For many of us- Anguela is an example of the balance, discipline and boundaries required for understanding and living life vision once you have accessed life purpose. As an adult indigo- learning to become empowered, learning to de-tangle herself from outdated conditioning, learning to live it, be it- in empowered life purpose. What is important about this case study is authenticity and focus required for self-discovery whilst maintaining integrity and clarity. The power of awakening can indeed begin to nudge us out of our familiar outdated self. The key is empowerment - balanced and integrity-based action. Discovering the peace within to honour self and life purpose. Holding life vision within the dynamics of others and the modern world is key and perhaps at times very difficult to balance. Anguela has spent many years discovering her life purpose and life vision, not only through study but through every person she met, indicating that she really needed to awaken to her power as healer in all that she created in her life. It is important to also consider the facets within our lives that demonstrate who we are. Once again, this case study highlights that you and only you, have the power to transform and free self into empowered life vision.

Life Vision Affirmations

- I know who am I

- I have clear boundaries

- I am living my life purpose

- I am in life vision

Life Vision Programme

1. Communication: Power And Strength.

Sit comfortably with eyes closed. Take five deep breaths.

Centre yourself. Visualise a column of light, of power. Which quality do you wish to bring to the way you communicate who you are? For example: stillness.

Take five deep breaths. Explore how that quality may feel. Explore the imagery of that quality. Expand what you feel. Expand the imagery you have visualised. See yourself communicating clearly in that quality. Expand the sense of/the imagery associated with that quality. Examples:

POWER, BALANCE, CONFIDENCE, PRECISON, HARMONY, COMPASSION

2. *Being In Your Power.*

To be focussed requires your attention and discipline. This is an exercise to strengthen your power and focus.

Sit comfortably and take five deep breaths.

Visualise or sense just what your power is. Focus on a vision of what your power is or could be. Feel this sense of power in your heart and body. Know it in your mind. Draw down a symbol of what your power represents. You can access this at anytime you feel you need to more conscious of being in your power. Examples: THE SUN, THE WARRIOR, THE TEACHER, THE HEALER, THE GODDESS, THE NEGOTIATOR, THE LISTENER, THE ARTIST, THE EARTH

3. *Positive Life Directions.*

Let your heart and mind expand. Take five deep breaths.

Write down all the positive qualities that are powerfully you. Take one beautiful quality. Expand into immense light. Connect with the quality. How can this quality flow and create a dynamic life direction? How can you utilise this quality to define who you are and express who you are in life? How can that quality touch others?

Take five deep breaths. See yourself being and expressing that quality in a life direction. YOU ARE POWERFUL AND FLOWING.

4. Connect with archangel Uriel. Archangel Uriel will expand the power of your mind and understanding of the power of authentic or divine self. A balance between soul and physical, heart and mind will be awakened. Archangel Uriel powerfully integrates these dimensions so that you can focus authentic self and life purpose, your life vision energy.

Archangel Uriel powerfully creates focus so that you can create who you are with precision. Uriel will awaken you to being the alchemist of you and your life!

CHAPTER 11

USING CREATIVE VISION

"It's been quite a trip so far, this crazy little thing called 'life'! A bumpy ride at times, with plenty of twists and turns, but never a dull moment. When I look back over my 35 years of human existence this time around it's wonderful to see how much I've changed in terms of my outlook. It just gets better and better! I'm often filled with a sense of wonder about life and it's myriad of possibilities.

I was a very sensitive child. My passions were (and still are) art, reading, writing and nature. I spent hours in my room making comics/scrapbooks/drawing or rearranging my 'nature' table - a hotch potch collection of abandoned birds' nests, deer antlers, fungi spore prints and fossils! However, I rarely felt alone. I had an incredibly fertile imagination and invented a whole host of 'imaginary' friends. I loved reading about faeries, ghosts, monsters, aliens and suchlike, sowing the seeds for my latter day fascination for the mystical/esoteric.

I had a very happy upbringing. My mother, in particular, was a constant source of love and support, whilst dad imbued me with a deep adoration for the countryside and antique/second-hand markets! By my late teens the burgeoning feeling that I didn't quite fit in with the so-called 'real world' came to the fore. I struggled at University to connect with like-minded souls and so began a period of intense exploration of my inner and outer world. After graduation I travelled around Australia, India and Indonesia, immersing myself in meditation, yoga and eco-activism. The latter activity led to a number of years spent living and working on organic farms, eking out a life of self-sufficiency amidst the beautiful but often harsh landscapes of the Australian outback, the mountains of Japan and rural Britain. Despite the peace, tranquillity and sheer loveliness of my environment I felt very isolated most of the time and hankered for society.

During this period I was also recovering from malaria, which I had caught whilst journeying in Indonesia. I became very introspective, consumed as it was by the battle to regain my health. This quest, married with the continuing search for life's 'meaning', paved the way for my interest in the Eastern philosophies of Buddhism and Taoism, as well as an increasing fascination in Traditional Chinese Medicine. Having had acupuncture and herbal medicine in Japan, I decided to train in these disciplines on my return home. I moved to London and embarked on a life of study, martial arts and, in a bid to balance out my overly serious early twenties, part-time DJing & 'glamming it up' on the dance floor. Around this time my mum started to develop her psychic abilities, after having blocked them for so long, and from thereon we had had a much greater understanding of one another. At last I felt I had a comrade in arms within the family!

In recent years I have felt much more comfortable with myself. I don't feel this need to fix anything. Indeed, I have been learning to love all aspects of my being, the light and dark. Concurrent with this shift in my mental outlook, I feel a stronger connection with the universe, a sense of belonging and a greater understanding of the 'interconnectedness of all things'.

I booked a session with Tracey because I wanted some guidance re-my soul contract/purpose. I felt that I was on the right path but that in certain areas of my life there were blockages. What Tracey said in the reading resonated within me on a deep level. She was spot on! It was like a cosmic kick up the arse and certainly different to any work I had done on myself before. Tracey summed up the essence of my being with the phrase 'you are a healer, artist, writer and psychic', encouraging me to pursue these activities with lusty abandonment. Furthermore, Tracey tapped into my love of magic and myth. It was as if she had a window to my soul!

I know that I've got the ability to excel at all of the aforementioned skills. However, Tracey's session has given me the confidence, which I often lack, to really go for it! I had been meaning to paint and write for years, but somehow never got round to it. After seeing Tracey I started painting almost immediately and haven't looked back since. Likewise, my writing has started to flow again, with poems literally manifesting overnight, as if plucked out of thin air. This renewed creative zest has had a knock on effect in all areas of my life. I feel more whole and there is a real sense of flow in my life. I also have more confidence, determination and focus to do what I want to do. A case in hand is the added impetus that the work with Tracey has brought to my fiddle playing. Moreover, I have enrolled in a psychic development course with Tracey, which has helped to build upon the positive foundations established in the soul contract session.

I am definitely in life purpose, but it is only the beginning! My self-belief is much stronger and I am very excited about the journey ahead.

Ethan

"**Your sensitivity is in place - there is a deep subconscious knowing towards healing. I want to still your energy. You are questioning whether you want to develop the psychic. This will help you with the side of yourself that has heightened sensitivity and emotional. A lot of your energy is being used constantly- you are being drained constantly as a healer who is psychic as well. You are ultra-sensitive - you can teeter into fatigue and ultra-stress. You have had this energy, this light, since childhood. It is not about saying I am going to develop as a healer, as a psychic - you have had this since childhood. You need to take the edge off your sensitivity by working with the psychic-being in control of it, managing it. That's what is going to help you so that you can work out the reasons for being you. This is all about the way you use your psychic ability better- much more effectively. There is a lot of opening via dream work but I want to make you more conscious. This will also make you feel quite tired. I want you to harness your psychic energy much more clearly. You are a healer first** and foremost so you will have to approach psychic work from that angle. You will not train in traditional psychic development. You need to find a way of supporting who you are within your psychic training.

Have you thought about doing tarot cards? This brings a fluidity to you - you are creative and imaginative. It will give you a confidence - working with fun, imagination, mythology and archetypes. Your imagination is your healing tool- that is what needs to be expressed. I don't see you working psychically in a traditional way- its about working with magic, symbolism, mythology. You want to connect it with healing. How it can heal people- your work has a feeling of potential- the magic of the esoteric so that it can be very creative. That's going to stretch you- your own creativity. How you explore drawing and painting. Then you will have the magic of both worlds. Your creative projects need to blend with the mystical. Bring the artist in yourself into the work you do. It will bring you into working with very powerful imagery - what mythology represents. How you learn to take the weight of what mythology means. Step into magic and how psychic can be a very imaginative tool. You need to become a psychic who works in many different directions. You are very interested in the magic and magic of alchemy in terms of what energy work is.

Within two years you have got this creativity. You need to paint. You haven't painted yet in the way that you need to. It will come through. You are a healer, psychic and artist. You need the fusion of all. Later work- developing through drawing, through painting. You have always known that you have talent - the contract is understanding HOW! How you lift into higher levels of energy so that you can manifest who you are. This is very much about how ungrounded you have been for so long. And how you can really pull down who you are on a soul level and that brings you confidence. There's a desire to work artistically, there's a desire to teach - its about finding the confidence to do so.

This has a mystical feel - creative, imaginative spiritual. You have been through your quiet, reflective spiritual phase but that's not really you. Not the quiet silent " I will retreat" - breaking away from the illusion of that. You have trusted that you are changing.

What must you do next? You need to turn around the fact that you feel old. You are on a cycle moving from more emotional to being more inspired - exploring writing- stories pitched to children. A decade of work where you start to master who you are. You've got the creative, you've got the imaginative, you've got the stories that are locked inside your head. You always connect with your inner child. You can be so eclectic and overjoyed in terms of what you do. Let's look at what we need to be writing and painting. Some room for you to explore abstract art. You have a lot of flair and freedom.

"Where do I need to be?"

Don't be the hermit. You need to be quite close to London on terms of your development. If you pull away - think about the new you coming forward – let's start work, let's start networking - you have social flair - people who have a lot of healing energy. You have to put the past in place - have you written memoirs in the past?"

"Yes, diaries."

"You can put your memories to rest - you can be dynamic and creative. Really show who you are - in the creative.

"I want to be creative again."

Your creativity is your healing tool. You would be a very good teacher - writing and story telling. You would be fantastic working with children. Making your imagination so much part of life. This magic is what you are trying to achieve. You are exploring the psychic, the creative. I need to share what my skills are and my imagination. You have flow in the next decade through to twenty years. It's about living your life in your imagination, creativity, intuition and healing- it's about being a fusion of everything. If you need to paint then paint. If you need to develop the psychic then do that.

Great grounding works with connecting with children. You never have to be lonely again. You are drawn to rural England. Have you been questioning more healing training?"

"Yes"

"This is a big decision. One where you are more serious and you need the wild you to step forward. There are financial considerations- you have to get this right. How you make it all work. Promise that you will create the space for your creativity. It is an extension of what you already do. There is also a question over how you bring your creativity into your therapeutic practice. Your creativity becomes more practical*."*

"I am an acupuncturist and trained in herbs and acupuncture. Working with that for three years. I want to go back and finish the herbalism course. I feel like I am stuck. I don't connect with the people. I work in Canary Wharf - I feel like I am not being me. I feel like I am trying to fit in. It's cutting out my creativity. People are too business-like."

"There's a Pandora's box to explore your creativity. You can look at the psychic and that will activate your creativity and imagination. The archangel you are connected with is Uriel - the root of your issues - your personal power. Your whole life is carried by your spirituality, your sense of truth and being committed to it. There is a strong sense of being physically affected by having those values - by being in conflict with other people with stronger energy. **You need acupuncture in order to learn how to make your energy flow - so that it's being positive in the way it benefits you. You are going to do high quality healing work.**

"I have some niggly health related issues."

"This links into your creativity. Stress, digestive issues, lethargy, dehydration. The stress is causing digestive issues - food intolerances - non-diary, non-sugar."

"But I have being doing Chi Gung and Tai Chi for three years."

"You need to write stories. Working intellectually - working with new ideas, writing. This will connect the creative with the psychic. I am also seeing you needing to work with people who really need healing. You are working with the wrong energies. Your energy is always better when you working in the most demanding of circumstances.

"I do feel that. I start to feel the symptoms of people I work."

Ethan, in his 30s, is a dynamic example of an adult indigo. His life vision expanding in all directions. The key here is balance - his life vision is an expansion of his sensitivity, spirituality and creativity; one he knew was essential yet very difficult to achieve. His understanding of just what these essential qualities (within him) was key so that he could anchor and focus his energy into a powerful life vision for himself. Sometimes a less focussed creativity can direct our lives in a far less dynamic way. Our lives are then directed into working with people who reflect how little we are connected with the most powerful sense of self. Ethan's power came to life when he began exploring channelling within The Awakening System which developed a life power tool and strong energy base so that he could communicate and create more. This really expanded his creativity both in writing and painting. This also expanded his true vision of self and just what he could achieve spiritually, professionally, materially and romantically.

Life Vision Affirmations

- I am free to create

- I know and understand my Soul Purpose

- I live my Life Purpose

Life Vision Programme

1. *Healing Emotions.*

Every time you feel low emotionally, it plays a powerful part in the quality of your physical energy and quality of insight. Becoming more aware of this level allows greater freedom and power emotionally and creatively.

Let the mind expand. Let the heart open. Take five deep breaths.

Empower your heart and mind visualising sunlight emanating from these powerful centres. Visualise or sense how you have been feeling. Just note this. Sense or see an image that can empower and energise who you are. This brings freedom and power to any emotional uncertainty. This brings greater power to emotional well-being. Let the image or feeling of emotional power surge through you. You can let go of uncertainty. YOU ARE POWERFUL. YOU HAVE CLARITY, VISION AND ENERGY.

2. *Creating Life.*

Let your heart and mind expand. Take five deep breaths.

Connect with an activity you would love doing. Expand in light. Surround yourself in the power of the sun. Visualise yourself doing this activity. Visualise yourself having the confidence to bring this activity into your life. Energise and expand this life vision. YOU ARE POWER-FULLY CREATIVE.

3. *Soul Power*.

Let your mind and heart expand. Take five deep breaths.

If your soul represented anything what would it be?

Take five deep breaths. Press your feet into the ground. IF YOUR SOUL REPRESENTED ANY IMAGE WHAT WOULD IT BE? Let the image gather power in your heart and mind. Let it flow through your being. YOU ARE POWERFUL.

4. *Creative Vision*.

Take an idea you wish to develop in your life or work. This is the seed for your framework.

Sit comfortably and take five deep breaths.

What image would you choose that represents your power? Expand this all around you. Honour the heart and the head.

Take five deep breaths. How does this idea feel? Can you visualise or sense this idea flowing in your life or work? Can you see or sense a place or framework for it. Where does it lead you? How do you sense it developing? What can it become? This may be a vision or a word/s. Does it feel right? Example: A painting. How do you see that painting? How could it develop? Where can you see this painting? In home, in a gallery? Example: A book. How will it develop? How do you see yourself in writing in one or two years?

5. Connect with archangel Uriel as symbol or name. Uriel is the alchemist- therefore a rapid life power tool- synthesising and inspiring who you truly are. The importance of power, precision focus is key to Uriel. Thus- expanding authentic self powerfully through so many more facets of your life vision. Archangel Uriel will provide the discipline and precision focus to deepen inspiration and creative vision. Uriel also

empowers with self belief. As the alchemist Uriel will allow you to achieve your creative vision rapidly into the modern world. Your ideas and inspiration quickly manifest.

CHAPTER 12

INTO AUTHENTICITY

"I had always felt strange, awkward and out of place. My earliest memory was the Shake and Vac TV advert and Bucks Fizz' ' Land of Make Believe' - that was my national anthem. I would sing and dance to anything and everything. I fell in love with music. Home was unpredictable at times, I felt scared most of the time. My mum seemed to be busy always at work or always doing something. But when she wasn't at work she would try to do things with us, like going to the seaside. My dad was a nice man (to everyone except his wife and kids) - but a violent man. I don't remember much time and encouragement from my parents - it was hard love tactics. My dad was always ' rule with an iron fist', and my mum is the peacekeeper.

I have two big sisters - they were like parents - and an older brother. The four of us had each other, and we always had a good time together. We all had a great sense of humour, laughing was our favourite pastime. My sister used to be a dancer. When my parents were out, the house turned into Studio 54.

That's when I discovered I loved to sing. Music was one of the only things at home that we all loved and enjoyed, especially on the first of January- my mum's birthday, they were the best times. But the fun would always be interrupted by anger and violence. I didn't receive as much as I witnessed. I just recorded it all with my eyes. I wet my bed until I was about eight, and always had nightmares until recently. I always wondered how we got here and who we really were. One day I was sitting in my room and I felt weird, I was looking at myself from across the room. I went downstairs and told my parents. They told me to pray and to forget about it. They told me to keep quiet or people would think I was mad.

I was watching Top of the Pops, Aztec Camera were performing 'Somewhere in my heart'. Then I heard a soft voice repeating, " You're going to be on the show one day".

My middle sister moved back home, she was acting a little strange and we discovered she was mentally ill. My sister was violent and would turn on all of us. I left Secondary School and went to college, I was never quite sure what I wanted to do, then I did nothing for a year, became depressed. I would cry a lot and felt like I didn't have a reason for being here. Then my sister had a baby, I spent all my time with them, we would play music and I would sing, then I realised what I wanted was to sing! So I found a music course, I started it, loved it and things started to look up. I was performing, writing songs and singing, for the first time I was doing what I loved!

My brother was Dj-ing and he had lots of friends in music, one of them influential. My brother took me to his studio. Some months had gone by and the track 'True' became big in the underground garage scene, there was talk of being signed to a major label. The song reached number four in the charts, we were going to perform on Top of the Pops. Everyone around me even my mum and dad were happy for me, except my boyfriend - so he finished with me. I was as happy as Larry, I was free. I knew the angels were taking care of me. I was happy but something was missing. I longed for my soul mate. It was December 2003 and everything was going great - going to fancy places and parties.

I went out with a friend in the West End. We were having dinner talking about relationships- and I felt sure my soulmate was out there. I told her about this guy I had met, he was nice but I had thrown away his number. When we finished our meal- I opened the door- who was standing there but this guy. Synchronicity. We started seeing each other. We released another single last year, I had found my soulmate but still there was something missing. Then in 2005, I started to feel low again, I wasn't working as much, had a few good things happening in music, but something was missing.

Then a dear friend told me she had been to see Tracey. She said, " She's the best- it was like she was reading from a book, she's different, she really knows!" Tracey told my friend something I had dreamed about two nights earlier. In all my years of being me and having lots of readings. Confidence- that is what has been missing. Tracey saw that I didn't even see myself properly I was lost for words (and that doesn't really happen, ever) it was like she was reading from a book, my jaw dropped a number of times, because the detail, the things she could tell me about me, resonated with me deeply. I didn't have any questions - in the end she answered every question I had in my mind.

The accuracy is something really wonderful. I am in wonder of her ability to be so accurate and so fast! After the Life Vision session I was ready to sign up for Tracey's classes. I have received so much support and healing working with Tracey - practical advice - that I can work with, I feel like I can do anything my heart desires. I must be in purpose. I am still working through my issues, I know what they are and how they affect my life, and I have the tools and the confidence to work through them. I know how to love myself better, I know how to love others and I know the feeling, whenever I am out of sync, I put my tape on and get back in line."

Hawa

Session September 2004

"You are learning how to express yourself more eloquently and energetically. You have a lot of work being done - you are more grounded; you have a little work to do on your self image - the way that you look; your self image - the way that you are desperate to be admired. You are also looking at how you develop your personality - to know it and own it. This comes as a direct result of your relationships - you are either too strong or too weak. When is there going to be a balance? You need to package up your energy. You are interested in the way other people package themselves - this connects with self-image - how you bring healing and spirituality in this.

You need to trust that you don't need to collect more and more

skills. You are learning to connect with truth. You have very good marketing skills as well. No more spiritual shopping - how you start to make this all work. You need people to work with - you come to life when you have people to talk to, people to work with. You have an instant way of working people - making them feel uplifted, positive. There is self-development within this – it's angled into supporting people in their lives as well. Lets get on with this - trust, market and streamline your ideas. Let's look at self-esteem, communication, self-development, how people visually look. You are looking at how people communicate who they are visually and spiritually. This is not about fashion design. Exploring how people present themselves and how they communicate that. You are also exploring how people express themselves. You have strong business skills. You should be connecting with people who need to learn how to express themselves. You are looking at developing a CONFIDENCE approach. The visual and the creative combined. You can teach and demonstrate what you know - terrified about whether this will work but also the financial. You need to market this as a professional businesswoman. This is about waking people to who they are, making people shine, your joy and laughter - getting people to laugh at themselves.

You need a creative outlet first - then your intuition will flow. Your life purpose is to look at the creative, intuitive and spiritual. I see this goes back to childhood. The psychic needs to be developed - quite seriously. It is interesting with you - you like people to come to you. You need to market yourself - how you set up workshops and seminars. You have to get the marketing right. You will be making moves in this direction by October. Your background and talent lies with trends. Your confidence will grow the more you develop it. Humour, healing, laughter, you coming to life in a workshop situation. Self-help books - it is not. You have read so many but never finish them!"

"I don't finish them but know the rest!"

"We have been steering towards this work - to make more money, to have more self-esteem. The more fun you have, the more you attract the financial. Approach this with what you know best - music, movement and creativity. Steer yourself in a more responsible way - this is business.

You are in a relationship that is on and off. This is teaching you about your self-esteem and the way you communicate. One of the few people who can put you in your place. This will give you a sense of harnessing you - recognising that conditions are required within relationships - integrity. This relationship is the best and worst. You have someone very different to you in terms of career. This will help you market yourself better and move away from being flaky New Age. Your New Age shopping trolley became too big! There is a question over home and living together. You are finally coming into a partnership that is inspiring your creativity. You need to recognise this. This contract is about how you are packaged personally and professionally. You have met your match - this is a permanent relationship. Don't drive this person away. You need to work passionately and professionally with the public that will neutralise your energy at home. You need this time free to finalise your work ideas. This is about where you belong - in your relationship - at home. This is about staying in London and if you need to run - then you travel with partner together.

Your father's energy has a very strong presence - your communication issues, your esteem issues and your intolerance to people."

"He is a nightmare"

"You need to move into being a woman. Father has to let you fly - in your business and your relationship. Your mother is completely different – self-doubting - you are also doing a lot of work on this. You have very little confidence and it is this where the important work is being done. You want to make links into media. You are turning your life around - you could have lived your life from your father's energy. You are developing a more equal love relationship - with dialogue and communication."

"I don't know whether I am lazy."

"You need to network professionally. Develop much more confidence - how you explore media - stretching your self. Music, in terms of writing, your creativity and work with people. Everything is there in your life but you need to trust it. This will only work if you make your contacts work for you. GO FOR IT!

Session November 2005

"There's an issue here of learning self-control. You are learning to surrender and allow events to take course. You are also considering your emotions and how you go with the flow - not highly analysing - you are highly sensitive. How you balance listening to yourself and make you more feminine. You can bring forward a softer energy - a more playful energy and if you have that for yourself then you have that with others. There is a lot of psychic energy needing to be worked with. You're feeling that if you don't use it you are storing huge emotions - making you get angry. The psychic needs to be dealt with. It's about looking at ways to express yourself in the right ways and slowing yourself down. You are spontaneous - it can cause you to have friction with people around you which you shouldn't have. This is all about your grounding. You have a question mark over home. You need space for yourself. You need many more creative people around you. People who are willing to support you. You feel very stifled creatively. Success is the key with you.

The issue is relationship - complexity. The contract here is learning about love. You are learning to be in your heart. You are the same as each other. This is about your grounding. Him - communicating and trusting. He is in a repeat pattern here - what is interesting about you - he can't push you aside - you are too strong. It brings you together. This is about home - settling down - feeling secure - feeling like you fit. You are looking at permanent partnership - marriage. This is about your confidence and believing that he is there for you. Marriage is being suggested within six months. All you essentially want is home and this relationship.

The career takes off once the priority of relationship has been addressed. You are blocked creatively. In order for your life to work, it has to include this relationship.

It has to include permanent relationship and it has to include home. Until you get this right - everything is on hold. You have to have the confidence to slow down. A different you is coming forward - more feminine. This will give you space to develop your work objectives.

Learn communication skills - this can come into your workshops - teaching dance. The visual side of you has to be honoured. You can make money with dance - this goes back to your confidence. Teaching.

What you want is a child. Your mother is very present. Very powerful. Make up your own mind about your relationship. Although you are strong, your mother's energy can obliterate you. Boost your confidence, not deflate it. You will be very good at working with young people."

"That's what I really want to do!"

"The workshops/teaching is with young people - creativity. The teacher - the supporter - boosting people's potential. This side of you is very strong - setting up a selection of workshops for young people. This can work very well for you. For you and this man - there is creativity in terms of music.

You need communication - not psychic, not telepathy. Use this powerful and intuitive energy in your teaching. This doubt that you have about yourself - you are working through to perform in front of people. You have to be more specific - teaching, communication and healing through your creativity. Entertainment. If you had the confidence you would look at musical theatre. Learn about the craft properly. You are essentially a performer."

"Stand on stage on your own. This is what your heart wants. How you grow in confidence. Voice work- how people speak- how people use their voices. Combine it with movement. Being really positive and inspirational for people who would not necessarily perform on stage. For yourself you need to separate the performer from the teacher. Your spirituality rests within your voice. Your partner supports your creativity more than anything else."

Hawa is another adult indigo who was thundering forward blindly into purpose and a life vision that screamed transform your perspective of who you are! At 28, Hawa found it increasingly more difficult to sustain performing confidence to the extent that her professional singing was on hold.

Acting with confidence was rapidly dis-empowering Hawa's life purpose. The Life Vision programme empowered Hawa's deep sensitivity and recognised her depth and power resting within stillness. This would also give her the time to deeply connect with self and assess exactly what she had to transform in order to be performer, partner and a vibrant creative . What an exciting time - Hawa can inspire all of us to discover the courage for self-discovery. At this time of accelerated awakening we can no longer perform behind a mask of who we are - painfully and tenuously just holding an illusion. As we are all probably experiencing at this time, to live in truth is vital. And to live in truth in emotional freedom is key. Confidence is not something we act but very much expands from the depth of who we truly are. It is 2007, Hawa is singing at the Royal Festival Hall, London with the London Philarmonic Ochestra and working with children.

Life Vision Affirmations

- I am confident

- I am still

- I am peaceful

- I am in my life purpose everyday

Life Vision Programme

1. *Powerful Sensitivity.*

Sit comfortably with your eyes closed. Let the mind still and your heart open. Let any areas of stress fall away.

Take five deep breaths. Empower and energise your body with an iridescent rainbow. Honour your sensitivity as a tool that can be extremely powerful. It anchors you to who you really are. Visualise how your sensitivity represents itself to you in your life. See this as a powerful image. Energise and expand this image through you. See yourself as powerful as you access the power of your sensitivity. Anchor this powerful image into your body, by pressing your feet into the floor.

Take five deep breaths and focus upon I AM POWERFUL.

2. *Being In Your Light.*

Let your heart and mind expand. Take five deep breaths.

Let your incredible and magnificent light surge forward. Honour who you are. Press your feet into the floor. You have the power to consciously anchor this power. See your light increasing, expanding beyond you, into your life and touching other people. YOUR LIGHT IS POWERFUL AND CAN FLOW.

3. *Opening To Love.*

The power of the heart is the most powerful of all. See or sense just how powerful the heart is.

Take five deep breaths. In allowing it to expand you allow yourself to love and to be loved. Let your heart merge with other hearts.

4. *Loving You.*

The power of loving you is important in your awakening. See or feel just how powerful your heart is - to energise, inspire and heal who you are. See the heart as vibrant, all powerful. See you alive in the power of your heart. See you alive and powerful in the activities you love doing, with the people you love and the places you love to connect with.

5. Archangel Michael. Connect with archangel Michael by name or symbol. Archangel Michael will powerfully connect you only with authentic self and a deep sense of your purpose. Allow Michael to become the visionary. Allow you to become the visionary of your life. Your life purpose- how is your life vision powerfully expanding?

CHAPTER 13

RECOGNISING YOUR INNER CHILD

"I have always been very intuitive, but the work has heightened every facet of my complex personality. The Awakening System is unique in that it taps into the very foundation of being. What I would also like to say is that it is far from 'New Age wave' which is way out there, and therefore impossible to integrate into every day life. The progress I have made with Tracey over the past two years is exemplary and extraordinary.

My life is flowing and I am constantly downloading information, outside of the class, which has enabled me to realise dreams at a much faster pace. As I receive the information I am becoming much more spontaneous and open to new ideas – in fact, embracing life to the full. It is very important to look back at the child I once was. I have always held onto the 'child like' spirit. This is the key to a happy life.

Brought up in a household with my grandparents, who doted on me as the youngest, I was blessed by being very much loved by everyone. However, the balance was sometimes out. We lived in London, backing on to a cemetery. The family worked, and therefore school holidays were to see how much mischief we could get into without being told off. One of our simple pleasures was walking with a bunch of flowers and visiting various graves. I loved to read tombstones. I thought deeply about the people buried there. Also, by living with older relatives, I experienced many deaths growing up. In fact, I often accompanied my mother to funerals, if the other family members couldn't get the day off work. I have always been very responsible in that way, and felt a responsibility somehow to those who have passed over. I have realised that my life is catalogued by who died, and I can remember dates, too. The biggest and most significant of 'The List' was my Grandfather, whom I adored. Right bang in the middle of A Levels, not good.

However, this start in life made me have so much empathy with other people in any suffering they were going through. It exposed 'The Healer' in me.

When it came to babies, I had no experience. I was happily married to a great guy and we didn't have the need. I was a very sound career girl, who was the Assistant to the Eastern Hemisphere Managing Director of a Houston, Texas Oil Company, based in central London. I loved the job and took all the girls under my wing that worked there. It was fabulous.

Then, one happy day before Christmas, we all took off to lunch, and my friend was killed by a bus. I was 25 and she was 23. This hurt so badly. How could this possibly happen? I was used to the elderly dying, but not the young.

Fortunately, I am married to a wonderful person who gave me unprecedented love, and I eventually got through the pain and grief, resulting in a beautiful baby daughter, two years' later, who I named after my friend. The birth was a trauma for me – but it was straightforward. 6 days later I had an out-of-body experience, which alarmed me. I had not experienced anything like this. I had not slept properly after giving birth, and the doctor explained I had just been on another level of consciousness.

The result was post-natal depression. This I had never heard of. All I felt was the huge responsibility of looking after this tiny little being, my baby, who was dependent on me for everything. I realised what a sensitive soul I was, and fortunately a friend came along to take me out of the house to a Yoga class. It did the trick. I followed this up by reading endless books on anything remotely associated with life and death.

Here we go again. Four years' later another beautiful, contented little girl. This time a pain-free fabulous birth. I couldn't believe the difference from my first experience as a new mum. With a wonderful life-style and a full weekly, yearly programme it just didn't happen, and it was pushed back deep inside of me. I was very people-orientated and followed courses in massage, aromatherapy, reflexology, homeopathy and the tarot cards. What I did do was become a Catholic because of the miracle of my girls.

I loved the Church, being inside, holy water and all the rituals it brought. I belonged. I had been looking for this since I was a child. It tied up all the loose ends that had been missing from my life. It has changed me. It was the balance between life and death that I had been searching for. I am the one that is telephoned to light candles for any occasion, be it a death, an illness, or a dilemma. It is a great gift to be able to call upon the hierarchy of Saints and Angels, and get answers. In that way, I feel this was all in the mix for eventually attending Tracey's classes.

It works in this way, IF you allow it to. Be open to the unexpected and jump in with both feet. You never know where you'll end up. I felt my life was back on course, again, but still the baby work issue wasn't resolved. I went back to work in London, which I loved. It wasn't as high-powered as I was used to, but I worked for my husband, so there were many perks i.e. being sent home after we'd enjoyed lunch and a bottle of wine! Great going.

It seemed that when I dreamt up an idea and saw myself doing it in a positive way, it would present itself! I'm a home-builder. I've been very happily married now for 35 years and interiors always fascinated me. I do believe now that your own home is a direct reflection of how you are feeling in yourself and how you cope with every day life. With that in mind I worked for ten years in interiors and it was inspiring.

The only huge cloud on the horizon at that time was the death of my dear friend, who was more like a brother to me. He died of a heart attack at 40 – his 17 year old son, my godson, tried to revive him in his own bathroom. It was dire. We were lost again – how could this happen when it should all be going so smoothly.

At that time I also covered Feng Shui, and space clearing. I am fascinated by energy and how it can be uplifting or spiral down into a pit! Believe me, I have seen homes I just wouldn't want to spend 5 minutes in.

The above led me to be head-hunted to manage a small hotel locally. A refurbishment was needed and I was drawn into a hell-hole of in-house bitching and fighting – none of which I found fun! It made me realise what terrible lives some have to endure, or don't do anything about, and I realised what a success I had made of mine, until ...

I left after two years as my cousin died suddenly at 23 – another blow, below the belt.

It was at that point, yet again, that I decided to give work up and have some fun with my 'young' grandmother. We shared everything together. She was MY sounding board for every occasion. She took the pressure off me. Always there for myself, my husband, my girls. At that time, I was prompted to look again – a little like 'Dick Whittington' – turn again, to the baby issue. I just happened to read an advert in a local paper and knew I would get the job.

It fell into my lap – a nursery nurse in a baby unit of a Montesorri Nursery. Hard work for hardly any pay, but I loved it so much. I realised then that right from birth, babies have their own unique personality. When you have 9 babies all lined up, so to speak, you can 'tune in' and 'read them' – like a book. My friends were up in arms – how could I possibly like a job where I came home covered in 'all sorts' and my clothes were fit to be burnt – this was not the person they knew, but I was so very happy. My grandmother was needing me more, so I left. How delighted I am now looking back that I did. I always remember an auxiliary nurse telling me she had given up her job to look after her ailing mother, just after I had had my first child. Her mother had since died, but I always remembered this advice. She valued the time they spent together at the end, which you can never replace.

So, three years later the inevitable happened. My beloved and revered grandmother finally went to meet up with her husband again. She was 97. How magnificent to have reached that age and to have been so loved by so many people in her lifetime – my friends, my family – in fact, everyone that came in contact with her. She is, and always will be, an inspiration and her spirit goes on.

It was the second Anniversary of my Grandmother's death. I came for a life vision reading in 2005. Immediately, she said you have 'midwife' all around you. I went home, searched around the internet, and there it was. I could become a 'Doula'. It's an American term, and basically it is helping mothers during childbirth and afterwards. Perfect. January 2006 I was on the Doula course (two months' later).

I am now living 'The Dream'. I love my job being with new mums, second time around mums, all problems, be they large or small, to do with babies. Who would have thought it. It has happened, at last! I have been given wonderful references from clients, and this is all because I am finally following my Soul Purpose. However late it presents itself, it is just that, A Present.

I am now training as a Birthing Doula. I am composing notes and printing off all recommendations about nutrition to help mothers have a painfree labour. I am going to include notes so that post natal depression is avoided. It is all falling into place. I love being proactive, disciplined and forthright.

We have a good group of Doulas in Hertfordshire and I have FINALLY arrived!!

Sue

Session March 2005

"You have a really humorous energy and you want to communicate and engage with people. The way that you listen needs to be as balanced with the way that you speak. You feel that the world is such a beautiful place and yet is such a storm. You are in two places-because you are not grounded then you move between feeling it's very exciting and safe to feeling the opposite. Reality check comes in through being anchored spirituality- you have always anchored yourself through listening to other people. Being the person who supports emotionally - the person who is always there to listen. You are now being challenged to be grounded without needing to be like

that. You don't have to operate in that way anymore - more humour, give and take - you have already decided this. The way that you honour yourself. You are essentially an energy worker. You have questions over healing and honouring yourself. You are very burned out. You are going to find some peace and stillness for you. You are going to be supported for a change - by spirit, emotions - a huge turning point.

Lets start with training immediately. You want an even-ness - you have been used so much as a stop gap for other people's emotions. You have a lot of time to give to people that concerns counselling. That's when you will achieve more physical energy. You metabolism has been worn down by stress.

There is heartache - it's a spiritual letting go. You have paperwork you need to let go of memories, your photographs. Look at key moments and photographs. You feel a huge learning curve. You have always wanted to support other people. You have had to learn how to rationalise why you hold emotional problems for everyone else. Coming into your purpose- fully conscious is part of the power. There is such a need to be heard. You need to honour yourself as a healer and teacher, the communicator. Find the physical strength to be in your purpose. You need to connect with the cultural activities you love - theatre, music and dance.

You need to be around people who enjoy the arts. This side of yourself has to be honoured more - the arts, travel, literature. You are very social. You need to be fed by vibrant people. Listening to music in particular is shifting your emotions. You need to spend a day in retreat with your music."

"I put Anton and also Les Miserables on the other day - I so loved it."

"You are moving forward very fast. You are slightly changing your approach to soul purpose. The physical health is being balanced as a result. You feel that you are tired. Look at the way you are feeling. There's a need to question your nutrition. The physical needs to be balanced. You need more exercise. You feel very sensitive at times and that can make you feel very emotional. There is a connection with archangel Gabriel. You are being driven towards healing work - empowering work. You have worked so hard helping others in your life. You have come to work with healing work at the right time. You are looking at what you need back - the playfulness, the laughter and how you are going to work with people.

Session October 2005

"You and partner have an excellent relationship. You get this right as a marriage, as a partnership - you are earthed, relaxed - there is nothing to worry about at home. Very much thinking about future - how you question spending more time together abroad - travel. You are renewing what your marriage is about. It's leaving you with space for you. You need to develop as a healer - connected into hospitals and children. You want to tap into a broad spectrum of children - children from all walks of life. You are feeling that it rests within hospitals.

You are very much linked to your friend and her child. So you are coming into to help both of them and her interest in healing work. This is a journey into different environments connected with children. With Teresa - she is also connected with Gabriel's energy. Healing work - look at how you can help the parents. How you can help Teresa and her son. The question is when - do the training now. You must do it now.

You will then have an amazing balance so that you can manoeuvre relationship and work with children. This is about working with children and their parents. You are interested in nutrition as well and working with children. You are wearing one hat- the medical and then working with alternative health as an advisor. You will have qualifications - baby massage, nutrition and parenting. You need the NHS and alternative therapies to work for you."

"I have always had an interest in non-conventional therapies."

"You are developing a business that is child-centred - with programmes of healing for children. Working from home. You are setting up information for children and parents. This is home-centred. This is a business that connects into organisations. You have training to do. Some practice into hospitals as well. You want to work with teaching people."

"I think lots of parents do it wrong with babies - because I got it wrong. With my first child - because I got it wrong with post-natal depression."

"Work with it through healing work and nutrition. This is about creating work that can help children properly - within the next three years. You have some voluntary work to do first. Find your strength through healing training. Nutrition sits very strongly with you. More travel - Italy. If you do a lot of travel it means you do not have to be too hasty with the project. You are building the space both physical at home. You are acting as a consultant - then you can set yourself up as a business person as well. Teresa would be a good business partner for you. Look at some child psychology and how parents bond with their children."

Sue has really awakened since working with the Life Vision programme. Sue has connected with the realisation that life is definitely fun. She has discovered immense insight, healing and the energy of creation. It is this she has locked into for herself and it's infectious in the way it expands to all she meets and connects with. This is true modern spirituality. In her fifties, her life had indeed taught her how to recognise who she really is - not defined by wife, or mum, or friend. Her whole life story as you read it solidifies her life vision today. It is indeed a tapestry. It is a life vision of healing - that might almost revisit the past so that she can heal her perspective of herself as a young mother. The life vision session pinpointed precisely just who she was and her direction in practical modern spirituality and healing. Sue is organised and disciplined but loving and excited in a life vision that is perfect for who she is. This case study will inspire the light within all of us to surge forward and awaken life and world vision.

Life Affirmations

- **I am empowered**

- **I am inspired**

- **I am inspiring**

- **I am healing**

Life Vision Programme

1. SOUL POWER. Let your mind and heart expand. Take five deep breaths. If your soul represented anything what would it be? Take five deep breaths. Press your feet into the ground. IF YOUR SOUL REPRESENTED ANY IMAGE WHAT WOULD IT BE? Let the image gather power in your heart and mind. Let it flow through your being. YOU ARE POWERFUL.

2. BEING IN YOUR LIGHT. Let your heart and mind expand. Take five deep breaths. Let your incredible and magnificent light surge forward. Honour who you are. Press your feet into the floor. You have the power to consciously anchor this power. See your light increasing,

expanding beyond you, into your life and touching other people. YOUR LIGHT IS POWERFUL AND CAN FLOW

3. POSITIVE LIFE DIRECTIONS. Let your heart and mind expand. Take five deep breaths. Write down all the positive qualities that are powerfully you. Lets take one beautiful quality. As we move into life directions, expand in immense light. Connect with the quality. How can this quality flow and create a dynamic life direction. How can you utilise this quality to define who you are and express who you are in life. How can that quality touch others? Take five deep breaths see yourself being and expressing that quality in a life direction. YOU ARE POWERFUL AND FLOW.

4. HEALING. Let your heart and mind expand. Take five deep breaths. Sense and visualise your physical body. Your heart and your mind. Take five deep breaths. Energise in powerful light. See your body. Feel your body. Connect with crystal in your feet, your legs, your body, your arms and hands. Focus upon the clearest crystal in your brain and spine. Energise in light. Take 5 deep breaths. YOUR POWER IS TO HEAL SELF.

5. HEALING EMOTIONS. Every time you feel low emotionally, it plays a powerful part in the quality of your physical energy. Becoming more aware of this level, allows greater freedom and power emotionally. Let the mind expand. Let the heart open. Take five deep breaths. Empower your heart and mind visualising sunlight emanating from these powerful centres. Visualise or sense how you have been feeling. Just note this. Lets take a sense or an image that can empower and energise who you are. This brings freedom and power to any emotional uncertainty. This brings greater power to emotional well being. Let the image or feeling of emotional power surge through you. You can let go of uncertainty. YOU ARE POWERFUL. YOU HAVE CLARITY, VISION AND ENERGY.

6. Connect with archangel Gabriel with name or symbol. Expansion with Gabriel is key in connecting you with divine love for self and the

world. This archangel empowers, energises and connects self through the heart- awakening powerful healing and self realisation. A creative, world vision is activated. You awaken the powerful creator and communicator within.

CHAPTER 14

CHANGING YOUR CONDITIONING

"I think this is a very honest account of how I feel. I had real trouble with writing an account for you in the last several months as like I said at my last reading with you I have completely lost faith. I haven't included 'my life story' as such as I am at loss right now. I feel isolated and not sure whether I have moved at all. As always before, and this time as well, it has been the effect of personal life failure. I have turned my life around yet again, this time consciously - I changed employment and lifestyle and home in order to get back to university. I worked so hard last year - academically (starting a degree in anthropology and psychology at Goldsmith's University, London) and professionally in order to be able to move into this direction. And almost 2 years' ago I met Michael, with whom I have deeply known in my heart we share what people call 'soul connection'. It went all the funny ways, yet exactly as you said on the last tape - it hasn't ended, on contrary to my 'strong decision' for us never to even talk again. You mentioned again the word 'contract'. Michael came last week to London and of course we met and of course the unbelievable 'home' and beauty feeling was there. As a result of what has been happening or not happening between us in last months I have done much 'soul searching' and thinking and I realised that in fact I love him so much that I even lost most if not all of my relationship phobia and fears of commitment that I didn't even knew I would have.

You see Tracey, your readings were always encouraging as well. Even the last time, a few weeks ago - I came to see you as I was totally down, I went through so much again in September/October. I have not been that bad in years! I could not deal with intensity of feeling abandoned (yet again) and the loss and not understanding why weren't we together - when clearly there is a connection beyond physicality. I went back to wanting to escape, only university kept me going. I wasn't expecting you to say anything about my relationship with Michael, as I really tried to accept it was gone - as a way of getting myself back on solitary track and surviving. When you mentioned him and the soul connection , although it honestly was unexpected, I went with it as a happy child. It gave me so much hope and security. And then he said he was coming to London. And he did and now it all seems gone again. It feels like if I was living my dreams in my head and the 'reality' kept pinching me and saying - wake up.

We spoke again yesterday and he told me he thinks about not wanting to fall again; about killing his feelings, etc. I understand that very well, but I seem not able to kill mine and if HE doesn't decide for himself there is nothing I can do. I am really scared as every time I go through 'realisation' of his lack of feelings or indecision I go all way down. I feel so much pain and fear. It's ridiculous. How is it? I understood I might be able to help people at same point with my work. I am working on myself but oh, am I really contracted to keep experiencing loss and rejection from those whom I love? Am I meant for LOVE? I thought I changed that? Am I free to choose anything? It was funny to listen to the tape from last year - you said already the he should come to London. What is wrong with me? We really could be two most happy people who are equally independent to do their own work. Anyway, you were always the only one who saw our connection in positive and light way. Please explain to me how it works. Can I change things? Can I influence my reality? Am I not to share love with people? Can I change things?"
Johanna

I included Johanna as a case study to highlight adult indigos. It is a time of powerful change and transformation where adult indigos must transform outdated belief system both around self and the world. Clearly, adult indigos can infinitely question everything. This also prevents empowered life vision. Johanna outlines the transition so many adult indigos face at this time in stepping into life vision and powerful life purpose and really utilising intelligence. The importance of adult indigos like Johanna and several of the case studies like Tony, Caroline, Lena and Hawa is that their journeys have been incredibly difficult and yet magically empowering at every stage. With each life direction the power and truth of the adult indigo is highlighted. Knowing and being in one's truth is key and yes, certainly, it is the power of truth that is painful and liberating at the same time.

Indigo adults are pioneers – ground-breaking yet practical in their journey to achieve a modern spirituality within the world. Every time, the power of the adult indigo is expanded, their life vision is directed to work between worlds and dimensions. The adult indigo will achieve the most practical modern spirituality and learn to fuse worlds whilst maintaining the deepest truth for understanding self and humanity. Johanna brings hope for the most sensitive and dis-empowered adult indigo. Her life vision is beginning to take on true purpose - and this in turn will deeply reflect and transform just who Johanna is as academic, teacher, communicator and soul. Understanding and living life purpose is perhaps more important to adult indigos than anyone else as the deepest feelings of lack of connection with self and the world can become unbearable.

Once an adult indigo is locked into powerful life vision, the adult indigo is vibrant, alive, inspired and deeply powerful. On a progressive note, the powerful journey of emotional transformation is an important one to maintain the most delicate yet powerful creation of an adult indigo's life vision. Sensitivity and integrity is key - maintaining the essential qualities to focus upon humanity to massively contribute to a new humanity and earth vision.

Johanna's case study draws upon powerful transformation and trust of life vision. Johanna has entered into an incredible journey of what is sometimes like discovery and yet not at the same time. As an adult indigo Johanna has a very exact perception of who she is and what her life vision is and will be. As she expanded into the academic she awakened love for learning. She powerfully expanded into vibrant empowerment that locked her into focus through the intellectual. This indeed gave her a great sense of truest belonging. As she began opening herself into a loving relationship once again the issue of power re-surfaced. She became frightened of just being. There is no doubt this relationship is an important one- it magnifies her fear of loss. The relationship is where her journey of self-discovery is most powerful and it is here she will expand into her truest sense of self.

This can be an important case study, not only in how fragile we can all be in life but the fear we must transform so that we can truly step into deepest power in every area of life vision. Especially indigos- must also become so much more aware that we also have to wait for transformations in those we hold dearly. In Johanna's case study there is no end to this relationship, again this signifies that we do create our own reality.

First session.

"You have always been guided by the spiritual - you have always been guided by higher levels of reality. Now you are feeling restricted by it. You are very psychically sensitive. You need to be clearer in terms of your energy. You will feel like you are out of control or you are going along with what everyone else wants to do. That is quite difficult for you and can make you feel angry. Your physical is changing a lot - how you look, your weight. You need to work with the power of your self. Work with Uriel. You need to link into higher spiritual practice.

You have always felt disconnected with your body because you are an indigo- your central nervous system gets affected, your focus, your motivation get affected. You are already highly intelligent and clair-voyant. You will be a communicator and that shift will balance your metabolism and hormones. You have contracted to develop psychi-cally. Do not challenge spirit. Uriel is the core archangel to activate core soul qualities. You have questions over where your life is going. The question of your potential versus your reality. There is a serious

side. You do not want to be with young people- intellectually you want to explore psychology and the meta-physical. You are learning how to speak to communicate who you are. You are even questioning why you are in London. For training and education.

You are learning how to consolidate who you are. There is the temptation to run away. You are getting a perspective on your potential reality. You are interested in shamanism. This can be creative for you. You're being asked to work with imagery - the Tarot, runes, shamanism - you are learning about history and evolution and applying it in a more archetypal - psychological - way. You are fusing two different areas together in academic research.

Your pathway has to stop being so emotional - this is where the research comes in.

You and your brother are like twins. He is very creative."

"He plays music."

"It is important that we talk about this sibling because your pathways are very similar. You are on the same level - the same spiritual journey though you are moving in different directions geographically.

You are learning how to negotiate, to communicate, and never abuse your power. Your life can be particularly painful at heart level. Until you find peace, love will be difficult. You are looking for the complete love of your life and this will not happen until you find peace within.

You are so much stronger than the men you have encountered. You haven't come into your spiritual power. This would take you into the events that would take you into relationship.

You are not in life purpose yet. You are tempted to leave London. You have strong links to South America and you want to train there shamanically. There is a strong academic link with you - esoteric studies with mainstream education. You are taking research abroad -

combining the travel, combining spiritual training in the right quali-fications. You need to start working on educating yourself - research that goes hand in hand with your interest in the metaphysical - anthropology and psychology. You are interested in cultures. You will understand the psychic. You are interested in how information is handed down through generations. You are also very connected with your ancestral energy and your psychic ancestral energy. You are also really interested in cultural roots.

You have always been demonstrative of your emotions. You have always been able to connect into other people's emotions. You have carried so much emotional energy even though you are quite young. Use the way that you have contracted to work emotionally with people to give you financial success. There are lots of questions over your potential and where you should be. The answer has been blocked so that you focus upon the spiritual and psychic. You will become a spokesperson. You need to go back to study- developing the academic- using the cultural differences to speak about. This has a lecturing side of it- you will be very at ease once you move through the study. You have a strong interest in history, culture, anthropology, shamanism- this is what you need to plan.

This is being developed in the next two years when you connect with a degree programme. You can bring in the unconventional and convention at the same time. This is mainstream. This is balanced. You will not be dominated by only the spiritual but the academic."

Session in April 2006

"You are not grounded. Past fear is still making you feel heavy. You have old emotions that need to be transformed. You need to state your power on an emotional level. You can be very positive or in despair. Your despair is cosy. You need some inner child work. You feel vulnerable and exposed. You don't want to do anything. You are even looking at your surroundings and you don't like these. You have taught yourself how to reject things. We need to stay connected to knowing that things can be perfect in the lightest possible way.

That links you into nature and trees. You have question marks over where you are living. You don't feel comfortable in the place you are living. Switch off the psychic when you go to sleep. You are moving in summer but you are certainly staying in the UK, in London. You need open spaces. You are moving June/July."

"Yes. Nothing has worked out."

"You are in massive inner child healing - rather like you don't believe you can be happy - and that needs to be changed. This is psychological. As soon as you start studying you begin to heal. Even friends - you need intellectual equals. You want to live alone. Study brings you into your positive pathway. You are also afraid of life running smoothly. You will get to grips with study. You want to prove yourself. As soon as you study that's when you start to fly. That's going to redirect your focus from self into the world. You move into anchoring yourself into this life.

You have to study - graduating. The study is building your energy so that you can become a communicator. You keep questioning healing. You are learning to communicate, to write and gearing yourself to the writer of books. By June /July 2006 you are cementing yourself where you belong in university. You will not feel the same sadness because you will be linking into areas of study that will excite- anthropology. You will use it to help people on a humanitarian level."

"I know I want to do social anthropology and religion."

Session in November 2006

"Really brilliant mental level energy - interested and dynamic, intelligent and alive. As we move down through your energy field, this is your insecurity - the way you perceive yourself. You need to transcend this - this will take you into the way you share your knowledge as communicator. This will allow you to become much better at holding your sensitivity, holding your energy, holding the issues you have about your self-esteem. Stay put in London. Stay strong - you are creating the right platform for yourself intellectually. This is your theory, your ideas - stretching yourself through teaching. The English language is starting to work for you.

You are in better shape - you are drawing your energy back from those you don't resonate with. You need to be stretched in your work. You need to work in a larger corporate environment - administratively - being anonymous yet respected within your own field.

There is also a question mark over relationship. You have a question over giving your heart. Self-respect is creating a big shift - to love, to be respected, to earn respect. You are starting to feel that you are home in London. The way you make money will connect you with the United States in terms of the academic. The States will give you a place to professionally fit - in learning environments. You have had to recognise that you have had to stretch yourself - into higher qualities - into your purpose.

Working with the mind will allow you to intellectualise and understand what love is far better. You are being asked to connect with your ex-boyfriend at Christmas. He has connections with Germany."

"He is German."

"There is a choice in terms of your connection with him. You are feeling happy about being in London. He is also obliterating the power of his father - becoming less significant to him. His father is dead."

Life Vision Affirmations

- I am powerful

- I am expanding my life vision

- I know who I am and my life purpose

- I open to love

Life Vision Programme

1.Loving You.

The power of loving you is important in your awakening. See or feel just how powerful your heart is - to energise, inspire and heal who you are. See the heart as vibrant, all powerful. See you alive in the power of your heart. See you alive and powerful in the activities you love doing, with the people you love and the places you love to connect with.

2. *My Life Vision.*

Write down your hopes and dreams for yourself. Write down your hopes and dreams as a child. What do really need to create in your life? Who do you need to connect with? You can also ask these questions after sitting comfortably and visualising you as powerful as the sun.

Take five deep breaths. Expand as the sun and open to your hopes and dreams.

3. *Insight.*

Expand in light through your body. Take five deep breaths.

This exercise will deepen your sense of clarity of vision and intuition.

Take a direction that may or may not involve another person. Expand the diamond of light in the heart and head for clarity. Ask a question such as: Where do I expand my abilities at work? See yourself very clearly in the work that you do at present or the work that you want to be in. Get a sense of possible avenues of development and growth at work for you. Which directions are highlighted? Ask a question in terms of how this can be achieved or developed in the best way/s. Write this down. You can always access possible directions and ask questions to refine your vision of how this can be achieved.

4. *Positive Life Directions.*

Let your heart and mind expand. Take five deep breaths.

Write down all the positive qualities that are powerfully you. Take one beautiful quality. As we move into life directions, expand in immense light. Connect with the quality. How can this quality flow and create a dynamic life direction? How can you utilise this quality to define who you are and express who you are in life. How can that quality touch others?

Take five deep breaths see yourself being and expressing that quality in a life direction. YOU ARE POWERFUL AND IN THE FLOW.

5. Working with archangels Uriel and Raphael ?. Archangel Uriel connect as symbol or name- will waken the authentic self- the infinite I at the highest levels. Powerful awakening and healing for an adult indigo is truly awakening divine power and authentic life purpose. Uriel allows perspective to anchor this. Archnagel Raphael connect with symbol or name- the infinite healer- will achieve deepest healing, expansion yet stillness for the indigo who can find it incredibly difficult to live in the modern world. Raphael expands multi-dimensional consciousness and a deep sense of divine and universal perspective and oneness.

CHAPTER 15

TRUSTING YOUR HEART

"Most people when asked say they cannot remember anything at all about or around their time of birth. I on the other hand am the exact opposite; I feel very strongly that I came into life with a thought fixed firmly at the front of my mind. The thought was and is, 'This is my Life'.

I know it seems odd but it is a thought that has, whenever I've been faced with challenges or had to stand up against being forced to do something I didn't wish to do during my childhood through to adolescence, popped up time and time again reminding me to assert my free will.

As a child I don't remember thinking much about life or life purpose as a whole, but I do remember having a feeling of self- assuredness, not in a brash arrogant way, just a very gentle quiet self-contained contentment, which meant even though I was insecure about the way I looked, I never wanted to be anything other than me, which I suppose is a huge blessing, being happy with your lot from the word go. Not to say that my situation was ideal, far from it, but nonetheless somewhere deep inside I still knew it was perfect for me. Even though I was not aware of it, my life purpose was always there around every corner; unfortunately I had a knack of passing the corners and wandering off down blind alleys. Time and time again I now realize that an unforeseen hand would come along to guide me. Even though I didn't know it at the time the one thing I loved more than anything else was singing, and everyone around me loved to hear me sing. I would spend Sundays with my mother going through her old records and singing along with her to songs by Nat King Cole, and Ella Fitzgerald amongst others, and if we watched a musical on TV I would spend the rest of my day singing the songs I'd heard whilst sobbing my heart out because I just loved melody.

My talent got noticed in infant school, and in primary school my music teacher approached my mother and asked her if she could teach me music privately outside of school hours. When I moved up to Secondary School the older girls would all gather round me and pay me to sing songs during break time in the playground. I was also known for my song writing. I would make up tunes and lyrics and sing them to a friend who would then tell others and before long people would be asking each other if they'd heard Lena's new song.

It's funny but at the time I didn't even see it as song writing it was just something I did for fun. Yet, even though I loved music I didn't see it as something I wanted to do. When asked what I wanted to be when I grew up, I would always say journalism or, I always had a fantasy of being in the army but only if I could be in the male corps being equal with the men. The other thing I yearned to be was a monk in a monastery not a nun because again there was something inside me that felt that the girls tasks would be easier and I was strong enough and brave enough to endure the same load as the men, or at least more than my fair share. An unfortunate set of circumstances led to me having to leave Secondary School a year early just before my exams. I had a year off and then went straight to college.

I signed up for a drama course but I really didn't like it so after a while I left and then drifted for a bit, much to the disdain of my mother and the rest of my family. During that period I spent lots of time at home singing along to my favourite songs until I could match and sing them note for note with whomever I was singing along to. One day by chance I bumped into a friend who belonged to a semi-professional theatre group, which staged only musicals; he asked me if I wanted to join. It sounded fun and so I said yes. The production they were working on was My Fair Lady; I auditioned and was accepted straight away. I was so happy and excited because even though it was semi-professional it was being staged in the West End. I was in the chorus and was even given a small speaking part. We had the original costumes from when it was first staged it was better than I could have ever imagined. It was here that the penny dropped, because, every time I sung everyone in the cast would say to me my god your voice is so beautiful you should be in lead. I was flattered of course, but finally, I started to hear what everyone was saying, and had been saying for most of my, up until then, short life.

So after that production was over I decided that I was going to do something about it and try to forge a career in singing. The funny thing is how obvious it had been to everyone else except me. I even bumped into a boy who had been in my class at secondary school, whom I hadn't seen for years and the first thing he said to me after saying hello was, "are you still singing?" Well, I was truly baffled as to how he could have known that I was now singing. But he said "oh, you were always singing in the classroom and in the playground" I just burst out laughing, as my journey up until then felt as if I had been all around the houses and down quite a few blind alleys before I got there, or here, whichever way you choose to look at it. Anyway even though I accepted that it was the right career for me to pursue I still didn't know it was my life purpose as I only saw it as something to do or pursue. I didn't realize that it was an intrinsic part of my being, but what I did know was, that now that I had found it, there really wasn't anything I'd rather do.

After a series of well-timed coincidences and a lot of hard work, I finally arrived at the point where I suppose anyone trying to make a career out of singing and song writing wants to be. I landed a recording contract. It was extraordinary after all; having a dream is one thing, making it come true is another. They say, "be careful what you wish for" and I now know why. I also learned that wanting something doesn't necessarily make you ready to receive it. I got everything I wanted, only it brought with it circumstances that I, being naive and headstrong in equal measures could never have expected, or been prepared for.

With all my choices from then on, I completely missed the mark. I was operating completely outside of myself. Instead of relying on my instincts, or trusting what I knew to be right, all the things which had got me there, I now relied totally on other people's advice. Whom, I now realize in hindsight never had my best interests at heart. I'm not blaming anyone after all that was my choice. I had begun to operate from a position of insecurity and fear. Where was my saviour? My life saving thought that I had been born with.

I had completely forsaken it and in doing so I was about to learn some very harsh lessons about life and human nature. Very soon my dream became a nightmare, one that I had created all by myself. Feeling completely disorientated and helpless it was at this point of appearing to have everything, but really feeling that I had nothing, and knowing deep down that there was much more, something else, that I decided to walk away and find out what it was. And so, henceforth I embarked on what I like to call my spiritual journey.

A journey which has been inclined to many stops and starts, although I know that within that, there really is no such thing, as it is a process which never stops even though, to the unenlightened it can appear that way. I can't really say where it began because even though I didn't know it, it began from birth. But at the same time wherever I am I always feel as if I am at the beginning, albeit a beginning of something new and great.

A few years ago a friend of mine who seemed to be so much more spiritually aware than me took me to the College of Psychic Studies. We attended lectures, and sat in the sanctuary meditating and trying to make connections. I had already had a few channelling experiences by myself but still I was convinced that she knew much more than me. After a while, I sort of drifted away from my friend, and the college, and got caught up in the external world again. But I always had the feeling that there was something more. After a few more years of what seemed like stopping and starting, a series of events led me back to the college. I was attending a course on developing psychic ability with an emphasis on being a medium when the teacher recommended that we attend a lecture of another sensitive at the College called Tracey Ash-Ingley. I had no real expecta-tions I just went out of curiosity, The lecture hall was packed to the rafters with other qualified mediums, psychic consultants and the like, and the air in the room was filled with excitement and heady anticipation. My curiosity rose. Finally the moment everyone had been waiting for arrived and amidst rapturous applause a beautiful, glamorous figure approached the stage. Her energy was light and totally uplifting, she wasted no time in sweeping everyone up in her positive flow it really was exciting.

Tracey then started to explain to us the purpose of archangels and how we could utilize them to enhance our everyday lives. This stuff was all completely new to me but I was becoming more and more intrigued. Could one really just call on archangels at the drop of a hat and have them assist you? Apparently so. The next thing that happened caught me completely off guard. Tracey explained that she was going to guide us all through a short meditation at the same time as calling on the energy of an archangel called Uriel, of whom I'd never heard. But, as I closed my eyes I felt an inexplicable surge in my stomach a kind of wave coupled with an overwhelming feeling of warmth and joy. With that my eyes filled with tears and I found myself embarrassingly and uncontrollably sobbing. I reached in my bag and found a tissue and tried to stifle my tears. She then spoke for a while and as she looked around the hall I caught her gaze and got the distinct feeling she knew what I was going through. Tracey then took us through another meditation calling up archangel Gabriel; again I had an overwhelming response. After the demonstration I felt lighter and drained at the same time.

I then decided to book a consultation with Tracey, which turned out to be brilliant. Without any input from me she proceeded to tell me all about myself and key points in my life. It was if she knew me or had access to my mind, I found it quite amusing really, the idea that somebody who has never met you actually knows more about you than you do about yourself. Anyway after my reading I decided to attend one of Tracey's' psychic awakening courses and ever since then the change in my life and the way I perceive things has been incredible. I feel so much more grounded and the anxiety I carried with me from day to day has more or less disappeared. I have since moved onto Tracey's life purpose classes and I can honestly say that my situation has turned around from being one of, 'if only I could' to 'when I do' my confidence has soared and I now fully understand how I've held myself back in the past.

Needless to say the stop-starting, which has impeded my progress for so long, is now truly behind me. I feel as if my life is full steam ahead and the most important thing is that I have a sense of being in control of what happens to me, where I go, and how I get there. It's a truly liberating feeling, which I could never have achieved without Tracey's gentle, accurate guidance. The lesson she teaches you regarding maintaining a balance between your spiritual life and your everyday existence is invaluable. As it is often there where the confusion lies. At least it was for me. I can honestly say now, with hand on heart and without a doubt that my spiritual journey has truly begun. "

Lena

"You are so sensitive - it is really difficult for you to hold your energy. Work with the higher energies - this will ground and anchor you. You have never been grounded - no matter how hard you have tried. You live - you have one toe in the world and the rest of you is other worldly. That's how you are - that's what you need to celebrate. You have a lot of energy associated with high frequencies - working with archangel Raphael. You have a beautiful voice. Singing. Exquisite - your voice is the thing that makes you come to life, it's the thing that you trust and the thing that makes you connect with being here. A lot of you can be pulled off-centre - but if you can stay true to your voice and your imagination and your spirituality it allows you to take a slice of this world to be daring enough to shape who you are! That connects you into writing as well. You have this whole spectrum that you can really work with and it builds your energy so clearly and dynamically. How you stay true to who you are. This is what your partner says - so what are you here for?!

This is your spirituality and your musicality together - working the two things constantly together. Writing and arranging music. This is about how you stay true to you. How you stay in charge - even though you can be the most sensitive person ever - you know that you can be successful. How you can create a connection between the ethereal and your musicality. This comes through in your writing and how you can give a different perspective. This comes through with your voice anyway. There is so much of your spirituality being bound in the voice – it's natural - all a gift.

You are always channelling. Your channelling is you working with your voice. The spirituality is there. You have inherited this. Your voice changes to suit the people you are around. It's natural. It's your being. You are playing with ideas about making what you do purer and purer. How you resonate with people - how you are coming into your own. This is about how you see yourself - drawing exactly the right people to you who can help you. This is about you being in the right place, at the right moment. The only thing you are saying is that you can't believe it as you usually have to unravel everything in your head. This is about flow - playing and collaborating with the right people. You can be seductive. A diva coming into your own - also as a woman - with the confidence to hold who you are. That sensitivity is still there but is being integrated with the person who can really write. The person who can really write is housing the sensitivity. You are being asked to integrate yourself psychologically – it's only psychologically. You feel everything is falling into place."

"I do. I am a lot clearer than I have been in my whole life."

"You have always had to torture yourself and cling onto reality and now you have got a very practical reality in singing. This is why everything is starting to fall into place. Up to October, you are easing your way into 'I belong'. You can collaborate with people - risking putting your voice out there - not being overpowered by anything else. You are using your instincts about who to work with. Live work - you are growing into it. Feeling fantastic about what you are doing and who you are. A really different you coming in. You are really coming into your femininity - the goddess - your sensuality and sexuality. It's going to give you a magnetic quality which will make you get noticed. You are earmarking yourself for success.

You are back on track. You will be given the success that you deserve. There is such a strong side that needs to connect with the States - live performance. You have also got a body of songs that are ready?"

"Yes."

"To work live - improvising and being confident enough to do it. It's not about needing to step out of your fears. It's time. You don't need guides and teachers to do it for you - you need to do it yourself. The only thing you have been afraid of is yourself. You are not afraid now. You have really changed. There is an opportunity coming with your work so that you can be seen - honouring yourself - live work and collaborating with people who love their musicality. You need two or three really good musicians around you. But it's your voice more than anything else. To be public - getting on with it! Working live in central London. There is nothing holding you back.

There is also a strong side of your self that feels isolated. Your friendships have to come from people who are musical. Let everything else go. You need people who love what they are doing - perfectionists. Raphael indicates that you can be so sensitive around people - this has made you feel like you have been on hold for a long time. You have felt like you have been hanging and waiting. From May last year 2005, you decided to be earthed - stepping into flowering professionally. You need to find someone you can team up with to perform live with.

Success comes with your voice. Don't trip over yourself by thinking too much. You are so powerful but you don't even know it. You don't need that many people around you in terms of friendships. Friendships will open through who you collaborate with musically. You love the rapport that musicality brings. You seem to resonate with strangers - with healing - your songs are very healing.

You have a male that is strong who can stand by you. It's taking you to where you need to go in your self. This is one person who can reach inside you. He is in your writing. He is waking you up. He is shaking you - bringing you to life. A soulmate connection - he is powerful in a really unobtrusive way. This is the depth that you have been looking for in a relationship. This person fits every dimension within you. You fit. The dynamics of this relationship will make your life purpose possible. Moving out of your limitations and you stepping right into your power as a writer. He is inspiring that. Can he help you? Manage you? He can push you - he feels the right directions for you. You need to be looking for his trust, his support."

"He knows people in the profession."

"He comes into your writing, your life purpose - he can harness directions for you. Sometimes you can be very stubborn. He lets you be you. He makes you confident in what you do. This is important in the way you cut your own deals and work on a business level. He is sharp. He can help you market yourself. This is good. You are both as powerful as each other. The relationship is very equal. You have been waiting for this balance. It's about quality of being - your soulmate and soul group. You are both accelerating the writer within each other. He is the key to your freedom. You need to admit that he is the one. Marriage. He sweeps you off your feet - let it happen. This is going to give you the power that you need as a woman, as a performer. You need his energy in everything that you do. Your physical health can nosedive because of your sensitivity. You seem to get strength from him. You need to be around more people like him."

"They are rare."

"You are meeting more people like him. You will network with people who are strong. It's about you coming into your strength and your power and this will automatically align you with this synchronicity. How you know your heart - what you need to be doing. You have to trust - be more of a diva in performing.

Lena has embarked upon an incredible and very independent healing journey that has brought most innate wisdom and self-beauty. Lena had spent many years in isolated spiritual discovery that brought her to a perfectly still place within. A perfect base and stillness to achieve spiritual perfection in self and her music. Her focus into the spiritual has left deep questioning and questioning of self - in terms of is she ready to really be? Her focus on the spiritual had also left her with deep concerns about her place in the world and the value she placed on herself around people who might be dis-empowering. Lena is stepping into her authenticity within the context of her deep spiritual self-discovery. The Life Vision programme has activated a modern spirituality vision that includes her in the world and expands her into performance. Her focus on self was essential so that she could recognise empowered sensitivity and work with her voice from her soul. She is now in her spiritual power to just BE. All of us will resonate with this case study - with each step questioning authenticity. The deeper we enter into self-discovery the more we uncover who we are and the more we expand into powerfully authentic life vision.

Life Affirmations

- **I am divine**

- **I am empowered sensitivity**

- **I allow myself to BE**

- **I am authenticity**

Life Vision Programme

1. OPENING TO LOVE. The power of the heart is the most powerful of all. See or sense just how powerful the heart is. Take five deep breaths. In allowing it to expand you allow yourself to love and to be loved. Let your heart merge with other hearts.

2. LOVING YOU. The power of loving you is important in your awakening. See or feel just how powerful your heart is - to energise, inspire and heal who you are. See the heart as vibrant, all powerful. See you alive in the power of your heart. See you alive and powerful in the activities you love doing, with the people you love and the places you love to connect with.

3. LIVING YOUR DIVINE POWER. Write down the qualities of how you wish to live your life. Select one to work with. Visualise what this is. Visualise how this may take shape in your life. Take five deep breaths. POWER QUALITY: CENTEREDNESS. How can this quality manifest in your life. Where in your life do you wish to develop centeredness? Visualise or feel what centeredness could be. And expand this. Take five deep breaths. Where could you bring this to your life. For example: work, relationships, modern life. See yourself bringing this centeredness to an area of your life. Examples: PEACE, INSPIRATION, ENERGY, HOPE, CONFIDENCE

4. MY LIFE VISION. Write down your hopes and dreams for yourself. Write down your hopes and dreams as a child. What do really need to create in your life? Who do you need to connect with? You can also ask these questions after sitting comfortably and visualising you as powerful as the sun. Take five deep breaths. Expand as the sun and open

to your hopes and dreams.

5. Archangel Uriel. Connect and expand with name or symbol. Uriel expands your spiritual vision and sensitivity into the modern world. Uriel will awaken empowered sensitivity. The key to this exercise is expansion of self on all levels- authentic self- right here, right now. Uriel will awaken a new vision of dynamic spirituality and powerful creativity.

CHAPTER 16

LIVING THROUGH BEREAVEMENT

"I was, according to my Mum, very difficult. When I was fifteen, she told me that I had come into the world screaming and had not stopped since. It seemed she was always angry with me; she disapproved of my disorganisation, my tendency to lose things and my liking for make-up and boys. I was harshly disciplined; my early memories are of being smacked repeatedly and of feeling generally misunderstood. I cannot remember a time when I was not afraid of life.

We moved several times as I grew up due to my Dad's ambition for promotion. I did not fit in and I began to be bullied. I was picked on for wearing unfashionable clothes, for having strict parents, for having freckles, for my early physical development at puberty and for not wearing a bra. I hated my new school and the people in it and was sick every morning out of fear.

My parents did not want me to go to the Secondary School where my Dad taught and I decided I wanted to go to the private school that one of the girls in my class was planning to go to. I liked the idea of this grand school with its castle and beautiful grounds and I was not keen on going to the girls' school that my parents had in mind for me. My Mum had to go back to teaching, which she wanted to do, but all her money went on school fees. I carried guilt about the fact that my Mum had nothing for herself and, as an adult I struggled to feel comfortable with spending money on myself.

Despite going to the school of my choice, the bullying continued, as my belief in myself as a victim, solidified. At one point my friends fell out with me and did not speak to me for a whole term because they decided they hated me. I was often ridiculed for my physical appearance and I recall the devastation and worthlessness I felt when, at twelve, I was voted the second most ugly girl in the class. My hormones were out of control, I had acne and scars, I was depressed, I had body odour, my Mum insisted that I wear sensible unfashionable shoes and my legs were too short. I never told my parents the full extent of my inner torture.

My one ally through my struggles was my brother, James. At some level I had known how important he was to be in my life the day I looked into his hospital crib after his birth, when I was two. He studied constantly and at school he did very well; I think I had a touch of envy but it was not enough for it to come between us. I talked to him about all my problems; he was more like a close friend than a brother.

When I was 16, my Mum found out she had breast cancer. She had conventional treatment and returned to her teaching job. Shortly after my Mum's diagnosis, dark hairs began growing on my chin and legs, a condition shared with my Mum though never spoken about and a further manifestation of my hormonal imbalance.

I scraped through my 'A' levels and the only course I qualified for was Primary Teacher training with music as my speciality. When I started college, I remember feeling depressed, disconnected from the other students and strangely homesick. I had no interest in partying and drinking or even boyfriends. Near the end of the first term, one of the girls in my hall of residence, who I didn't know, was asking for someone to fill the place of her friend who had dropped out of the ski-ing holiday they were going on in December. It made little sense that I would consider going on holiday with a stranger, but I did and it would later prove to be one of the best choices of my life. At the last minute the original destination of Andorra had to be changed, as there was no snow. We chose to go to Austria instead.

On the first morning at breakfast I noticed someone sitting at another table. My friend and I got talking to him and I knew I liked him. That evening our knees touched under the table and it felt electric. Nevertheless, we each thought the other wasn't interested and he ended up kissing someone else. Something in me knew I couldn't let this opportunity pass and I confronted him. We admitted our feelings and the *connection was undeniable. During that week I had a sense that this person, Jeremy, was my soulmate and he dreamt that we got married. I did panic at the prospect of commitment and intimacy and almost broke it off. However, there must have been forces at work ensuring that we got together; we later discovered that we had both originally booked the same hotel in Andorra and when this was cancelled we both chose the same hotel and destination out of several other possibilities. On returning home we began a long-distance relationship and with it began a healing journey.*

I managed to get myself through the first year of college and then was able to change to a three-year degree course in music and educational studies without having to repeat the year I had already completed. This left me with only two more years to endure at college. During my second year I had a dream that something was wrong with my Mum. When I phoned, my Dad said everything was fine, but she later found that the cancer had returned on the other breast. At Christmas she had the lump removed but never really recovered. By the following October the cancer had spread to her bones and liver and she had only a few months to live. I spent a lot of time home from college looking after her and actually I did come into my own at that time. I cared for her whole-heartedly. I suppose I was still trying to get her to love me. On my brother's eighteenth birthday my Mum said she had done her duty now. Two days later she died.

I got married in the summer after I finished my degree. I was so obsessed about getting everything perfect for the wedding that I developed irritable bowel syndrome, a condition which continued for over ten years and which worsened every time I was fearful of something. We moved to Bristol and I began a year's training to become a secondary school music teacher because I didn't know what else to do. I was not cut out to be a secondary school music teacher. Although a good violinist, I was not musically gifted. I was hopeless at the piano and without this skill, I constantly struggled to provide a good model of what I was expecting from the children.

At the time of my Mum's illness, James had become interested in yoga, meditation and crystals. I had dismissed it all as being weird. After Mum died, James went to University and during this time he became unwell getting headaches, fatigue and odd purple marks on his body. He became convinced that he was possessed by entities as he could hear their thoughts that were different to his own. At the same time, he told me that there had been unusual happenings in my Dad's house where Mum had died; the kettle would boil without being plugged in, doors would slam and he had a sense of being watched. He felt that my Mum's spirit was in the house unable to move on.

When I told my Dad he admitted that he had sensed things were happening and he was clearly afraid that Mum was not at rest. A while later, Dad remarried, put the house on the market and moved. Late one evening, a week before my Dad's house was due to be sold, I got a call from my brother; he was standing outside my Dad's house afraid to spend the night there on his own. He came over and the next morning Jeremy, James and myself went to the house. As I walked through the door, the energy felt so oppressive that I got a headache and there were cold spots in certain areas. Then, when the three of us were gathered in the kitchen talking about Mum the table moved about an inch and banged itself against the wall three times. I was freaked out. James arranged for his crystal healer friend to come to the house and do a clearing.

I woke the next morning feeling as if a burden had been lifted. When I visited the house, it was completely peaceful. Mum had moved on. This encounter with existence beyond the physical marked the start of my journey into myself.

That summer James went to America to work for a computer software company. Over the next few years we almost lost touch as James immersed himself in corporate life and left behind his spiritual practices .On my twenty-eighth birthday I wrote my resignation from my job with no idea of what I would do next. I wanted to find a healer who might be able to help me with my pre-menstrual problems. She told me that she and her husband were starting a healing school in the UK in September based on the work of Barbara Brennan. It was what I had been waiting for. During the first healing, I was amazed to experience a strong throbbing sensation and flashing lights at my third eye. The following month all the pre-menstrual madness was gone.

In September I began the part-time three-year diploma at The School of Energy Healing. I did supply teaching to pay for the course. In the secondary schools, I was frequently confronted with uncontrollable, abusive teenagers, who would riot in the classroom. As a temporary teacher who had no relationship with them, I didn't have a hope achieving anything positive. Whereas I found I enjoyed working in middle and primary schools.

In November 2000, I received an e-mail from James, which said he had a problem. When I phoned he told me that he had had two operations six weeks apart, each time to remove a grade four brain tumour, the most aggressive type and had been given only months to live. I could hardly speak; it was one of those moments that you think only happens to other people. I flew out to Washington to be with him. We visited healers across the States and rode an emotional roller coaster; it was difficult to cope with James' dark moods combined with my own fears. Whilst in a bookshop in Asheville, a book fell off the shelf about shamanic soul retrieval. I bought it. The healings were not stopping the progress of the tumour and I couldn't believe that James would soon be gone. On his twenty-seventh birthday he lay in bed almost unable to walk. I thought he would die quite soon and I asked him if there was anything he wanted to do with the time he had left. He said he was really interested in shamanism, the subject I had been reading about.

I found a weekend course nearby. Jeremy had recently arrived to help me and the three of us went on the course. The shaman who ran the course was keen to work with James. I needed to fly back to England to do my healing course, so my Dad came out to look after James. During that week he had a healing with the shaman. Miraculously, the next day James got up on his own and walked around Washington. Later he told me that the shaman had performed a spirit extraction, energetically removing a spider from his head. In the weeks that followed, the tumour began to shrink and James was well enough to return to work.

In June 2002, eighteen months after the shamanic healing, my fears were realised; James called and said the tumour had come back. They were going to operate again. He had seen the shaman but it had not helped. I persuaded him to come to England for a week to see if any healers here could help. He came, but he was going downhill quickly. He went back to the States to have surgery after which he was almost unable to speak. Dad went to look after him with the intention that he would later bring James back to England.

When James came back to England I told him about Tracey Ash and he felt he would like to see her. He had a reading even though he could barely communicate. That summer was tough on the whole family, watching James' physical deterioration, addressing his need for medical care and the painful fight with his inner demons. He held on to life for longer than he needed because he knew I didn't want him to go. Late in the evening of 26th August, my Dad phoned to say that James had passed.

When I walked into his dimly lit room I felt this huge energy that pervaded everything. I did some healing work with the intention of ensuring his soul passed fully over to Spirit and I knew he was going to be alright. The next morning I awoke with these words in my head, "Make peace most of all with yourself. You do not have to suffer. Negativity is an illusion." I had heard that one of the first things a soul does on passing is to impart the wisdom they have gained to their relatives.

After James' death, I tried to set up my business as a healer even though Tracey's reading had suggested that I needed to focus on self-healing first. My ego pushed ahead to prove myself, but not surprisingly it never took off; few people came and when I did work I gave away my energy and took on all their issues. For me, working with adults and doing hands on healing work was tedious.

At school, I still found it impossible to be at ease with myself when I was with the other staff; I felt I had nothing in common with them and I would exhaust myself by unconsciously giving away my energy when I interacted with them. It was this, together with the fact that I wanted to try some healing work with children that made me decide to leave my job in December.

After giving up the teaching work, I was frustrated at depending on Jeremy financially; I did not have the energy to be in the world, yet I was bored at home. I had always been plagued by a compulsive need to have everything perfect, especially in the house. With so much time on my hands I became more neurotic; I wanted total minimalism and I obses-sively got rid of any possessions that weren't absolutely necessary or beautiful. Whatever changes I made, I was never satisfied and I felt tormented even by having to look at my surroundings. By August I was pregnant and terrified. I had such intense nausea that I was unable to get out of bed. I could not bear to look at daylight or colour so I stayed in a darkened room. I remembered that Tracey had said homoeopathy might work for me now that my energy field was more refined. My homoeopath gave me a remedy to deal with the fear and within a few days the symptoms had passed.

As with everything, I worked obsessively towards achieving perfection. Jeremy and I went to hypno-birthing classes with the aim of releasing my fears and attaining a pain free birth. I watched videos of women birthing calmly and without fear, I booked a birthing pool, paid for an independent midwife and intended to have a lotus birth where the cord is left attached to the placenta until it drops off naturally, giving the child a gentler introduction into the world. Yet, as the birth approached, I became increasingly anxious.

After twelve hours of labour at home, my midwife decided that I was not progressing and I needed to go to hospital; it was a deep transverse arrest and the baby was stuck on my pelvic bone. Malachi was finally sucked into the world by Ventouse extraction. However, every part of my being was hurting, I felt regret and that I had somehow been violated. In addition to being physically drained, suddenly I had this little person who needed my attention all day and all night. I did not cope well with the demands of motherhood and I put extra pressure on myself trying to be perfect. I was so obsessed with trying not to mess him up that I gave too much and exhausted myself.

Despite resolving many issues, I was still physically exhausted, unable to sleep and very depressed. Malachi wanted me to spend every moment with him so I almost never had time for myself. I tried putting him in a nursery for a few hours to give him some outside stimulation and me a break. He found this very traumatic and was so upset he would be shaking when I collected him, so we gave that up. The future seemed black; I could not envisage any work that I could be bothered with and I believed that Malachi could not handle being left. I felt so low that I would cry inconsolably for much of the time; Malachi would stroke me in an attempt to make me better. He showed such compassion but he also struggled increasingly with his own frustrations, and despite Jeremy and I working together to give him clear boundaries, his tantrums had become uncontrollable.

In August 2006 Jeremy caught the end of the Channel Four documentary that featured Tracey Ash; we had always intended to take Malachi for a reading with her because our earlier readings had given us such accurate and useful guidance, so with this reminder I arranged for the three of us to have life vision sessions. By the time I got my session with Tracey I was feeling desperate. I believed that I had done everything possible to change my pattern of collapse.

I was excited at the prospect of moving to Somerset; we knew we felt at home in that area. We now had the conviction that our new life was possible and I was eager to get things moving. I immediately put the house on the market. We sold within four weeks. Had I listened to my intuition and Tracey's reading, which had said we would move in six to *twelve months, I would have realised I was trying to push things too fast. This was nicely reflected by our buyers, who wanted us to complete very quickly and then pulled out of the sale. From time to time I lapsed into a depressive state, not seeing how we could ever afford the kind of property that Tracey had spoken of, which would cost double that of our present house.*

Over the next months financial help appeared in ways that I had not foreseen. I started to enjoy the process of manifestation being guided by the archangel energies I had learnt to connect with through Tracey's meditation work.

Since going to Tracey's monthly consciousness group and doing her 'Matrix' workshops, I have begun to learn how to channel, effectively accessing accurate information for myself and for others. I had done channelling before, but working multi-dimensionally in this way accesses a lot of information quickly. Although I had experienced the highest divine energies before, as Tracey observed, I focussed on psychological work. This is where I felt naturally comfortable, processing stuck emotions from the past. However, because I wasn't working from the soul level or with the higher energies at the same time, I stayed stuck in a never-ending cycle of healing issues. Therefore I rarely had any awareness of my higher purpose or the ability to move forward into my life potential. I now experience a tangible connection with the archangel energies, helped by the sacred space at Tofte Labyrinth where the Earth energies really support this work. I can ground effectively into the physical, doing this from the heart centre where body meets soul, rather than using the lower charkas. This proper grounding has allowed me to achieve the focus that Tracey had said I needed during the very first reading she gave me four years earlier.

With Malachi now allowing me time to do things on my own, I enjoy meditating daily and I have found that, as Tracey predicted, whenever I do purposeful spiritual work my depression dissipates and I feel connected to life again. Developing my psychic abilities, using the help of spiritual beings and working with the Matrix, has allowed me to be more accurate and to access a wide range of information that is totally specific to me or to the person I am reading. It has provided me with answers that I have been searching so long to find.

This work has given me confidence in the truth of what I am accessing; Tracey's insights and teaching have given me the ability to trust and to have a faith that has become stronger than all the nagging doubts. As a result, I have more energy and I function better in my daily life. If I do collapse momentarily from giving away my energy, I can sit using the techniques from the Awakening System to get re-centred and then continue living in the world. This in turn impacts on Malachi, as Tracey had stated, "When you feel fine about yourself, he'll feel fine about himself." Our relationship is healing and developing all the time. Each day I am touched by his compassion, his gentle healing energy and his beauty as well as his stubbornness and unwillingness to accept any injustice. With my improved frame of mind I am able to appreciate his quirky ways and crazy humour.

Our readings came at exactly the right time for us. I truly do not know what I would have done if I had not had that guidance to help me out of the hole I had got myself into. I know we will move to Somerset and that I will have another child and teach again, but I am less attached to things having to work out in a particular way; as Tracey noted, finally I can "stop thinking that everything has to be perfect." I am beginning to live the life that was always my soul's potential and I am doing it along side those of my soul group, whose purposes I know to be lovingly woven into one another.

Carolyn

Session in June 2002

"In the last six years there has been a massive amount of emotional clearing. You must trust spirit. You need to look at healing - it is the

most important move forward. You need independence. You also need to learn to ask for support. You can see energy. Your role is healing - more healing in the next five years. You are interested in regression and hypnosis."

"This is part of my training."

"It is a strong area for you. Strong visuals when you work with past life work. This highlights your psychic sensitivity. You have periods problems."

"I have never had a regular period in my life"

"There is physical healing too. The hormonal imbalance makes you too sensitive, too imbalanced, too erratic. Your body is being repaired- balancing of the hormones. There seems to be too much intellect- focus upon the psychological- too analytical. This will make you a much clearer channel for healing. Your breath needs to be slowed down. Meditation that is more shamanic- you being one- at one with nature. You need to be much more focussed. You are in a purification process at the moment. I feel there are issues of anger- let it out. The inner child is kicking and screaming. As a child - really angry - tantrums."

"I was dreadful as a child. It was always there."

"You have a huge issue of being dis-empowered. Yes, you have light but how do you work with it? You are resistant to strong male energy. You refuse to see spirit in this life. Let go of the " I blame my parents". Your parents have created pillars of strength. You have a vast light energy versus your inner child issues. You will have periods as well. You are very reluctant to acknowledge your femininity. You recognise what is happening. You have the ability to expand in channelling and mediumship. These are important avenues to develop. Your voice is particularly healing - communication.

Every turn in life you take needs to be a slow turn - delicately and sensitively made. Your energy is delicate - you can enter your healing clients' emotional arena - this is powerful not weak. Your partner has a lot of energy. He is very healing for you. It is a strong, unique partnership. You complete each other. The key to your relationship is talking. You can reach each other deeply. He is teaching you how to do healing work in a very different way. He is a soulmate. He helps you to recognise who you can shoulder in terms of problems. There is a gentleness and warmth. If you need healing be with him. Tone down the experimenting. He can be a teacher for you. He opened you up like no one else. Because you are so sensitive you misread him. Feel safe, feel your sense of power as a woman. You can balance each other out. You have the same issues. He needs a child - to fool around with. You will be ready for a child within three years. You will enjoy this too. You have patience with children. You will have a son.'"

"I am a teacher"

"A lot of healing, again for you, with this child.

Your brother, you have a role in healing him - helping him, letting him go. He is in pain. His eyesight is failing. There is so much pressure. You are both healers. He is transforming energy and spirit. He is close to your husband. He has a real sense of knowing other dimensions. You are really linking with what is happening to him - experiencing what is happening to him. He needs to be with you - to live with you. There is a super link - a telepathic link - with him. You will assist him. He is very psychic and pure in spirit. You are much closer to him than anyone else. You have to find the strength to do this. Part of his fear is about abandoning you."

Carolyn's son, Malachi, age 3 years and her husband, Jeremy, Session 2006

"Malachi is slightly not grounded. He thinks quite intensely. He is advanced psychologically. You are recognising his sensitivity. He has to be more grounded. He can ground through food - what he eats. He needs to eat nuts and raisins. He needs foods high in iron and vitamin B - bananas. He instinctively knows these will anchor and ground him. He has quite strong psychic sensitivity. He needs a nightlight. He is really susceptible to energy - to feeling - and that can make him not express himself even with other children. He can be swept along with how other people can be feeling. You need to get him grounded. He is a strong, intuitive healer as well. He is drawn to people. He also has a really strong sense of himself spiritually. He needs to learn how to read really early. He needs to be more focussed. Simple things will make him grounded - reading. He seems to have more of an attention span for reading than art. He is quite conceptual -he likes words; sound. He has psychic sensitivity. Mum is exhausting herself because she thinks she has to protect him from everything. Instead of you doing it with your healing techniques you are doing it psychologically. You are playing the mum who is putting up barriers for him. He has such a strong energy that you are never going to be able to hold him. You need to let him be free in himself. The sooner you can let him be - the easier it will be to handle him. He can be difficult. He is a child who will not be told what to do - you have to negotiate with him. He has his own voice and strength in the way he communicates. You need to learn to make this easier. You are trying to protect him because he is sensitive. I don't see him as being weak. The more you let him have freedom - the more powerful he can become. It is a different way for you. You have questions over you doing healing work. This will give you a different energy outlet. That will take the pressure off you being everything to him. This about how you open doors for yourself

- spiritually, practically and also you are tired and you don't know why. You need to slightly shift your energy levels and you will be fine. You are also thinking about having another child. This is *about taking the pressure off yourself and him (Malachi).*"

"All he says is baby, baby!"

"He can speak and communicate. All three of you have that. Another child will balance the family. You need to look for the small answers to making life perfect. You will make your mind up in the next three months. Stop thinking everything has to be perfect. Malachi, is a child who won't be controlled. You have to learn to live with it. You are giving him the space to explore who he is."

Jeremy

"You're feeling slightly sidelined. You are feeling in limbo - psycho-logically. You are thinking whether Carolyn needs some help psycho-logically. If you step back, you already have the answer. You are looking at how isolated Carolyn feels. You can push her along. Giving her the confidence to move in the right direction. You are being the healer in this. This is emotional more than anything else. She feels depressed and lost. Every time she feels like she is okay - this is associated with death. She perhaps requires some psychotherapy around this. The two deaths in her family need to be dealt with. You also need to move. A house move would help Carolyn shift. She is in a place where she knows she doesn't have to be who she used to be. She is in this transition - part of her doesn't believe that she can make the change. That's what the dilemma is - she keeps shifting between the two states - being really positive and happy. She does have every-thing that she needs. She needs to retain this reality without falling back into feeling like she is alone. There is a big question - where you live.

You are looking at a complete change and move - how you re-invent yourselves. A move is going to bring up Carolyn returning to teaching as well. She needs to do this - be around kids. Early springtime, next year 2007, everything will fall into place. The ideas need to come from you. You want to live in a place that is very rural and has a sense of community coming through it. You are not sure where to base yourselves. You are looking at changing what you do as a job. You either move into the midlands or the south coast. Somerset. Your work needs to change - the way that schools are run. You need to take the next step in terms of your abilities. This highlights the financial with you. Carolyn wants the same things. You work with technology. You need to come to life in a different way. You are looking at career options to make your life easier - on an adminis-tration level in education."

Carolyn - Activating Your Life Purpose

"This is all about moving. That's where your major worry is - you need inspiration for this and it needs to lock into the spiritual as well. What is interesting - a strong connection to Somerset. Your partner is thinking about what he needs to do as regards to his work. That also brought a very strong connection into education for him and how he needs to look at himself as far stronger in his career prospects and what the next five years will be for him. He is looking at a bigger financial package. You are both connected into teaching. Both being able to work and how your partnership works as well. You have to find a way of working together so that you both come into purpose in your own individual ways. Both of you healing, communicating and teaching. Him on more of a demonstrative level - training. You as a teacher - focus into primary. You are deciding upon this in the next six months. You are looking at Taunton. You are living in a village environment and village school. Your healing work will come into teaching children. You will do more healing than doing formal healing work with children. You will finally make closure to the past. July is a difficult month. You need to leave your house. This is associated with your brother. I think the person that your son is seeing is your brother."

"I was confused I wasn't sure if Malachi was my brother. They are so similar."

"James, your brother, is bringing forward how sad you are - to comfort you. You stroked his hands as he passed over. Massaged his hands. He doesn't want you to feel that you are alone. He brings teaching to you. Did your mother teach? Yes. You need to go back to teaching and work with it in a positive way for them - your brother and mother. This will draw closure on the past. Hormonally - you still get affected - linked with depression. You have to come into an inspirational job so that you can use the healing and psychic together. It brings you into working with kids. You don't want to work with adults. The sooner you start teaching the better. That's what is going to get you back to life. You need to be free with your fabulous soulmate. We need to get the move right, you back to teaching and that's what is going to shift everything for all of you."

"Somehow I am allowing Malachi to dominate every second of my existence."

"Reinforce positive thinking and Malachi will start to feel more secure. You need to start focusing on where you live and where you want to work. You are tired. Your present home in the past represented a healing perspective. You are looking at moving in the next six months. You are looking at jobs first then home comes in. Your

brother is very present because he knows what you need. Your son has his strength of character. You need to separate them - Malachi and your brother as individuals - and this will be a huge relief."

"He said that he would come back as my child."

"James is directing and guiding your life purpose."

The Life Vision programme worked with this family. It has been an incredible journey of several years where I have witnessed so much healing and transformation for this family. Malachi was the key - the accelerator for Caroyln and Jeremy - for partnership and parenting. Malachi - such a powerful soul and reminder of the power of James - a deep spiritual wisdom that always endures. Carolyn indeed suffered incredible bereavement that was excruciating in the light of her desperately low self-esteem. The Life Vision programme helped her to turn this perception around. Psychological alchemy is key. Freedom and healing is crucial. Carolyn has turned her life around after years of pain and focus into self-healing. Their lives are free. Malachi is free. Carolyn has taken deepest responsibility for herself and the role she can play in loving her partner and son. Freedom from fear is such a vital concept to consider in this case study and Carolyn and her family encourage you to reach into self and transform it. Once again, this takes you into a place where the power within transforms.

Life Vision Affirmations

- I am healing

- I am in the moment

- I have freedom to be me yet I belong

- I have freedom to create a perfect life vision

- I love who I am and beyond me

Life Vision Programme

1.Connecting With Self And The World.

Take five deep breaths. Let all of your fear flow down. Let the earth take it and neutralise it.

Press your feet into the floor- become physically aware. Visualise standing on the earth. As you visualise, stay body-aware, stay focussed. Connect with archangel Gabriel - expanding your energy through the heart, expanding all through you. Enforce that you are standing in your own spiritual power and you are actively working in your life purpose.

Take five deep breaths. Expand this and know that you are expanding into your potential.

2. *Inspiring And Energising Life Vision.*

You are drawing upon the highest energies as you connect with Gabriel.

Take five deep breaths. Affirm that you are healing and teaching and working truly inspirationally with communication in your life. Feel and know your energy expanding - your life vision expanding. The energy is flowing down through you and powerfully into the world.

3. *Activating Intelligent Heart.*

Focus upon transforming your body into clear quartz crystal. Your feet, legs, body, arms and head. You are expanding, you are opening to the highest energies of Gabriel. Your heart centre opens and re-balances.

Take five deep breaths and focus into the heart, feel your heart expand and transform.

Take five deep breaths. Connect with Uriel to bring powerful alignment and clarity. Connect with the infinite power within - your soul.

Your heart and mind can locate this. Focus upon your soul power expanding as golden light through you and beyond you. Your breath energises and expands this powerful expanding vision.

Take five deep breaths. Just be.

4. *Into Powerful Life Purpose.*

Expand in a pyramid of light. Take five deep breaths. Affirm that you are living your life purpose. Affirm that you wish to let go of limitations.

Take five deep breaths and connect with Archangel Uriel. You can quickly and easily access your own power. You are activating a powerful pyramid of golden light to step into for powerful transformation and energising.

5. *Connecting Mother And Son.*

Expand into a powerful pyramid of golden light. Take five deep breaths. Connect wth Uriel.

Visualise your son in his own powerful pyramid of golden light - he is empowered and happy. Connect with a deep sense of your soul power. Recognise how that energy can nurture and support him. You can work with him in a very different way even if you are not physically present. Honour his independence and his power. He will feel deeply empowered and supported.

CHAPTER 17

OVERCOMING FEAR

"I was born in 1958, I have a brother who is 21 months younger than me. I would say he fits a lot of the descriptions of an 'Indigo person'. We were very close as children, being able to read each other's thoughts a lot of the time.

My parents were a difficult pair. My dad was very unpredictable and although he wanted to get close emotionally, he didn't know how and had to cut himself off being incredibly needy. Mum was the strong one in their relationship and with us. She is still alive and also very cut off from her emotions. You can almost see a wall of shyness and fear around her.

Before I could speak I learnt to smile to make people think I was happy. That way I got praise. Inside I was scared of upsetting people, especially my parents who rowed all the time. If I was happy then it couldn't be my fault that they were angry. I rarely got angry as a child unless it was with my parents or brother. Eventually I stuffed my anger down. It manifested as eczema (from 1 month old) and asthma when I was about 14. When I was in my late 20s the eczema appeared mainly on my hands but it was so severe that they had to be bound for months at a time.

At school I never thought I was good enough. I was told by a music teacher that I would be doing O level music. I was terrified that I would fail, I got a B grade. I honestly believed that because I wasn't as good as the other girls I couldn't possibly be good enough. I have always set myself up against other people's achievements and convinced myself that I shouldn't even start something because I may not be good enough. This is a deep rooted pattern that my body gets sick as soon as I start to succeed at something. It is also exhausting. I either run around with masses of energy or collapse in a heap.

I started studying Shiatsu when I was 35. The course took 3 years and I found it very tough but at the end of it I had started to realise that I found something I am really good at and that I can develop in a way that works for me. My teachers gave me excellent marks and I had to stop myself thinking they were talking about someone else, or just being kind. I love this work as I can be true to myself when I am doing it. I don't have to pretend to be something I am not.

I fell in love for the first time when I was 18. We got engaged 2 years later and broke up when I was 21. That's when I decided to run away to Australia. I had started to save money when I was 18 and at 23 I had enough to make a world trip. I joined a group in Pakistan and we travelled by coach across the north of India and ended up in Nepal, where I met a friend and we trekked for a week and then went to Thailand for another week. I then went on to live in Australia for a couple of years. I began to realise, that because I was still so attached to my past, it was tough making new friends and in the end I wanted my old friends around me again and the familiarity of England. The trip taught me to be independent, and for some reason I had needed to go to the other side of the world to work out, that actually, I felt most comfortable with S.E. England. When I was 25 I returned to England and studied typing and shorthand to widen my job opportunities.

I fell in love again when I was 29 and got married to him a year later. He turned out to be an alcoholic and I finally got out when I was 37. During this time we lived in the North East of England, near Hartlepool, for 4 years. While I was there I met someone really special. I became friends with a lady who is very psychic and all of a sudden a lot of psychic people came into my life to guide me through the next stage of my life. It was fascinating. I received acupuncture and shamanic journey therapy and did several workshops. I started my Shiatsu training. Before I left my husband we had moved house and area several times.

It took a lot of courage to extricate myself from my life with him but when I returned to London on my own, thankfully, trusted friends and family were all really supportive. I have been lucky with their loyalty. I was in debt to the tune of a few thousand pounds but I had my sanity back.

It had been a very dark period lasting 9 and a half years.

Just over a year later I had got myself out of debt and was starting to be in contact with psychic people again. I was able to afford to do more workshops, and I had a shamanic soul retrieval. I also met my present husband too. An incredibly exciting year.

We were married when I was 41 and when I was 43 gave birth to a beautiful little boy. It was a very difficult time because he was six weeks premature and an emergency caesarean birth. We were so lucky that although he was small he was perfectly formed and healthy. He was in hospital until he could feed. I went through my normal pattern of thinking I was a terrible mother. I was anxious for the next 4 and half years.

Then I had a reading with Tracey and it was such a relief to be told that it was okay to get in with my Shiatsu and start being in touch with therapists and sensitive people again. I started to attend her channelling course each week. From the first week amazing things started to happen to me. I had phone calls asking for treatments, about two new people each week for the next month. They also rebooked, which had stopped happening for a while. I was much happier and less stressed. My family became much happier and my little boy stopped being so ill so often. Previously, when he was ill I used to have instant stomach upset and would need to be near a loo for at least 24 hours. This didn't happen and I didn't knot up inside. I also had a tremendous fear of him vomiting. Recently when this happened I just dealt with it and was able to be there for him instead of rushing off myself.

To be calm has been the most liberating thing for me. My natural instinct with people's energy has been heightened and I am able to trust that it is right, even if I don't know why, at the time. I have had to use my inhalers a lot less and my breathing has been a lot easier. The visualisations have been fantastic for me. I didn't think I would be able to 'see' anything. Each week I have got something from the sessions that have got me a little nearer to fulfilling my life purpose. I have also done a two day workshop called The Matrix. I came away with a very valuable lessen on how to hold my power in my everyday life as well as my work.

My main aim at the moment is to get myself known as a Shiatsu practitioner. I have been working with an artist friend to design a new logo. I think we are finally there and it makes me very excited to see these new colours and design. I will be continuing with the course again and have found that during my six week break my breathing is not as good and my energy has started to come from my solar plexus causing slight stomach discomfort. It is not as severe but I am aware that things could slip right back to where they were if I don't raise my energy levels again.

Isobel

Session in June 2006

"You are taking the next steps in a very thoughtful and structured way for yourself - writing helps you to answer your own questions - that on a channelled level could work very well for you because you are very strong mentally. You need to find ways of anchoring your energy for yourself. You are great when it comes to working with other people. When it comes to applying this to yourself, you keep on sabotaging yourself. Writing can create structures and goals for you. This is important - how you take care of yourself, how you nurture yourself, how you meditate, how you look after yourself.

There is a lot of rushing on a practical level. There is quite a need for you to externalise who you are through your home. How you are now recognising that you want to stretch yourself a lot further. You have a lot more headspace for yourself in the home - all about base, anchoring and home. This provides a strong foundation for you to work with the higher energies.

In terms of any healing work, learn how to conserve your energy in a practical way. You also get pulled into other people's problems. That healer side within you - you can get drained very easily. You need to reclaim your energy. Your energy needs to be contained in home. Draw boundaries around yourself. You need to be in control of your energy field. Your thoughts travel with people. You need to get disciplined with this aspect.

You need to write - list what you value in yourself - you need to stretch your self-esteem. You have to work hard on yourself, working on your physical energy, working on your self-esteem so that you have a strong inner core. This is what will allow you to come into being a very powerful healer.

How you compartmentalise your life areas so that everything is right. Perfection in every life area - this is possible but all you need is a little more physical energy. The home is working and then that allows you to step into the role of healer that is also spiritual at the same time. Your spirituality at home is through communication and your spirituality outside is expressed through people - how you perceive them, what they need on a healing level. These two areas have to be in place for your energy to be balanced. You will manage your heart energy better - open, expansive, creative, spontaneous in the home which is equally powerful on a healing level as you work with a difficult client. You seem to attract people who are physically low. You need your home to be correct then the outer work - healing – can fall in place. Your strength is reinforced by home. You have been trying to be too much. You become grounded by getting the home element correct.

You have been so restless - where do I take my energy? What do I do? You would be very good working with people with food intolerances, chronic fatigue. You are looking at how you make your work change.

You need to become all of these aspects - home, perfect partnership, the community, your healing work. You are also interested in teaching healing. This will make you feel valued. You want to be respected in healing. Again, this is about confidence - then you pull back. You will move forward - how you can value yourself, materially, financially as well. You are starting to surrender to your role at home, your role as partner - you don't need to tend to this so much. In terms of you coming into your power so much of your life purpose is bound in your confidence - to learn about your confidence in a supporting and gentle way. This is all about your key healing issues - trust and actually recognising your power and what that stands for.

Equal balance with your partner. The next stages - you being asked to mould the next stages - a new space to work in - where do I need to take my work next? September is a key month - more freedom in terms of the way you create a career - healing. Using techniques to develop re-energising techniques for clients. Write and market yourself - see that you fit. Package yourself precisely. Re-launch what you do in a new way. Empowerment. You are interested in quality of healing. You are also interested in diet, nutrition, well-being - take short courses to support your existing work. The only thing that is blocking you is purely psychological.

Surrender to your pathway. You need to be practical, busy. Link your work with doctors - market your self."

"I want to work with doctors."

"The bodywork and energy work will eventually combine in the next two to three years. Stay conventionally orientated – in health and GP centres. Each aspect of study brings you into a great sense of your self. Sense of yourself is key - the key to your freedom - this goes back to where you live and a conventional approach to healing. Your sensitivity has to become empowered. You need to work from a higher level. Your power will start to come back. Healing at a much higher level. Look at how you can be sensitive - yet powerful at the same time. Create the right healing space at home. You want to develop psychically as well."

"Yes."

"It will also give a stronger sense of your self. It will tighten your boundaries and on a personal growth level will help to shape who you are. You are already working psychically on an emotional level. Archangel Uriel is the one to work with."

Isobel is a case study who will resonate with every woman on a journey to re-claim her power from the first day she could remember. Isobel has indeed grown - coming to a vital place in life where loving husband and son, the family, is considered first. Yet again, this is a case study that asks Isobel to achieve more for herself, her family and her world vision. Her passion as a mother preparing a solid emotional future for her son is key. At the same time her passion as a healer - as a shiatsu practitioner - was also needed to be considered. The key is home, work and life balance. Isobel resonates with many of us. What is key here is the power base and soul-confidence to recognise that life vision can be created more dynamically than ever before.

The key to the Life Vision programme was maintaining power and confidence to hold and create this new life vision that would hold home and a professional healer's life. Again, it is vital to recognise and use the power of precision and the mind. What is also vital is the power base - without this in place magic and miracles fail to create and transform your life vision. The life vision programme gave Isobel the tools to expand and energise beyond - this allowed her to reach into the wisdom of her potential and recognise that she could create everything in her life.

Life Vision Affirmations

- I am powerful

- I am moving into confidence

- I can create a dynamic life vision

- I am empowered healer

- My dreams will manifest

Life Vision Programme

1.Positive Power.

Take five deep breaths, closing your eyes and being comfortable.

Let the mind still. Let your heart still. Visualise a powerful and positive image of you. It may be being healthy. It may be being powerfully creative and inspired. It may be living a life of pure simplicity. Sense and know that image is anchoring in your physical body. You can feel it in your heart and know it in your mind.

Take five deep breaths. Allow the image to expand and flow through you and into your life. You have the power to be this. I AM POWERFULLY CREATIVE IN MY LIFE.

2. Power Centre.

This exercise will centre and anchor you. It will give you a sense of who you really are and the power of that which is you and your life.

Take five deep breaths. Sit comfortably with eyes closed. Press your feet into the floor. Allow yourself a powerful awareness of the physical body.

Press your feet into the floor once again.

Sense every part of your body. This is your physical. You have the power to access and honour it at any time. This can happen by consciously focussing upon your physical body. In your heart, know who you really are.

Take five deep breaths. Feel the strength of the power of your heart. Let it increase.

Take five deep breaths. Feel the strength of the power of your mind. Let it expand.

Take five deep breaths. Visualise or sense your powerful inner core or centre. Let this increase and sit powerfully in your physical body. Visualise what this power centre looks like. It may be an emerald, a star, a sun or a painting. You are in balance. YOU ARE A POWER CENTRE. You are anchored in your life.

3. *Work Vision.*

Write or draw the power qualities of you in work. Or the qualities you wish to create in work.

Take five deep breaths. Closing your eyes and sitting very comfortably, take one quality into each session. Expand into the power of the sun. Visualise or know that this quality is expanding within. See or recognise that this quality can expand beyond self into your work relationships. Into, how you operate in a group. How, you network. Or, how you create work. Examples: CLEAR COMMUNICATION, INTEGRITY, CREATIVITY, FLOW.

4. Connect with archangel Gabriel in name and symbol. The creator-awakening the creator within you. Gabriel will powerfully radiate who you are in a modern world vision. Empowering you with a confidence to create and communicate who you are. The perfection of who you truly are is key. Gabriel also wakens the power of the divine feminine. Expand a white, radiant circle all around you.

Connect with archangel Uriel in name and symbol. Expand a white triangle within the circle you have created. Focus upon connecting with archangel Uriel. As the alchemist, archangel Uriel will awaken expanding authenticity, spirituality perspective and vision and empowered sensi-tivity.

These two archangels will activate powerful union of consciousness.

CHAPTER 18

DEFYING DOCTORS' DIAGNOSIS

"For thirty four years of my life, everything had been almost perfect. However, there was no religion or spirituality in my life. I had had no concept of, no need to make contact with my spirituality. I had no questions. There was nothing spiritual about my life. Thirty-four problem free years came to a grinding to a halt with the diagnosis of an incurable illness. I had been ill with laryngitis which had been slowly getting worse when, in November 2004, my father died following a long illness. Then in January 2005, my grandmother died. I was just coming to terms with these events when in February 2005 I was diagnosed with an extremely rare, incurable illness - Anti-Epilgrin Mucus Membrane Pemphigoid (MMP). The average age for someone with MMP is about sixty five so along with the rarity of the illness, it was no wonder it hadn't been diagnosed for eighteen months.

The symptoms were eighty percent ulceration of my larynx and pharynx and blisters on my face and torso. What made things even worse was that my doctors knew very little about the illness as there is less than one sufferer in every million of the population so all they wanted to do was to put me on depression inducing steroids for life. On top of that, I was told that my eyesight was would get worse and I would, maybe, even go blind.

It was a relief to find out that it wasn't throat cancer. However, you then concentrate on the word 'incurable'. It was a strange feeling of relief, almost. It was clear my body wanted me to stop working. I didn't listen for eighteen months so it eventually took the decision out of my hands.

So what was my alternative? I had to go within to cure. Eventually I made an appointment to see Tracey. Although, I had to wait a month, something inside me, told me not to see anybody else. So on March 5,

2005, I sat with Tracey and the first thing she said was, "Wow- you have an amazing amount of psychic energy". She said that I had been psychic all my life but had denied it because it scared me. She added that I had abandoned my creativity and although my personality was far too dominant- it was my spiritual side that was getting stronger.

Pandora's Box had been opened and at last I wasn't scared of my psychic abilities any longer. On 11 April 2005, I started the Psychic Awakening programme with Tracey and on 6 June, I started The Awakening System Programme. After the diagnosis, I hadn't gone through the 'why me?' stage because of how bizarre the diagnosis was I knew that it had happened for a reason. The doctors couldn't help me, I was on my own and what Tracey did was show me the tools. I could heal myself if I listened to me. I could find all the answers. When I was diagnosed, the doctors told me it would take at least eighteen months to get the condition under control. On March 3, 2005, my throat was no better but by June 21, 2005, my throat was 100% clear and I was told I was now in remission.

No doctor could now diagnose MMP. I made the choice- I would not go back to working on city trading floors and I would follow my life purpose.

From the experience I have been through and the results of The Awakening System Programme, it was clear that my purpose is to be a psychic and healer. I continue to train. Tracey gave me my power back. In terms of healing, she gave me the confidence to listen to my soul - to hear from within - to get that connection to self, back. It was so quick - the true me. I had always been using other things to be me. Basically having a very successful career in the city, I had never had what you call true basic self-esteem. Like most people I hid behind external symbols of success. What I really liked was once Tracey had unlocked what my problem was she gave me the tools to work with. My journey has been physical, emotional, intellectual and finally spiritual. She understood me. She helped me to do it for myself and to hear from within. From a sceptical capitalist in the city I am now working towards training as a healer. My life purpose is to help people.

I believe everything happens for a reason and finding The Awakening System only confirms that more. Unlike anything else Tracey shows you reasonable and versatile tools that you can use again and again that empower you. This means you never become dependent on her or anyone else. The fact that my body came up with such a bizarre illness that was so rare was a massive sign for me. I just had to understand it. It was like I had been set a challenge - it was probably the only set of symptoms and definitions that would have really motivated me to find my true life purpose!"

Charlie

Charlie refused to have his life vision session typed.

Charlie is a thought provoking case study- in the way he recognised his search for self- discovery. His journey into self healing is essential to understanding and tackling his illness. With integrity, he began facing his deepest healing issues as the only route to begin healing his illness. Not only this - Charlie has used the wisdom and empowerment of his journey to firmly help others. His journey into an MA in Spiritual Psychotherapy will lead him in so many exciting directions in terms of consciousness and the power of the mind.

What a difficult yet fabulous journey – from his passion for living- being purely the excitement of career and making money into the infinite power and understanding of mind and soul. This has been absolutely key in the way Charlie faces his healing journey. What an essential meltdown of values, of belief system, of the 'old Charlie'. Charlie gives hope to all of us for when we feel obstructed and encourages us to know that power and healing is within. Once again we are responsible for what we create, heal and transform. Once again this case study highlights our life purpose is our most valuable healing and awakening tool of all.

Life Vision Affirmations

- I am healing

- I have the power to seek new life directions

- I have the power to transform my life

- I accept the transition into new self

- I am always discovering powerful life vision

Life Vision Programme

1. *Life Vision.*

This exercise will anchor a positive life vision.

Sit comfortably and take five deep breaths. Close your eyes. Let the light of you really move forward. You may visualise the sun. Feel your whole being alive in this energy. This is who you really are.

Write down how you would like to see your life being created. Start with one life area. HEALTH. See yourself as being powerful and vibrant in increasing health.

Take five deep breaths. Write down what you need to achieve this. What will support you in your life?

Take five deep breaths. See your health being firmly anchored into your physical body. You are surrounded by powerful light to support you. Know that you will attract the right situations that will powerfully support your health.

2. *Power Centre.*

This exercise will centre and anchor you. It will give you a sense of who you really are and the power of you and your life.

Take five deep breaths. Sit comfortably with eyes closed. Press your feet into the floor. Allow yourself a powerful awareness of the physical body.

Press your feet into the floor once again. Sense every part of your body. This is your physical. You have the power to access and honour it at any time. This can happen by consciously focussing upon your physical body. In your heart, know who you really are.

Take five deep breaths. Feel the strength of the power of your heart. Let it increase.

Take five deep breaths. Feel the strength of the power of your mind. Let it expand.

Take five deep breaths. Visualise a sense or your powerful inner core or centre. Let this increase and sit powerfully in your physical body. Visualise what this power centre looks like. It may be an emerald, a star, a sun or a painting. You are in balance. YOU ARE A POWER CENTRE. You are anchored in your life.

3. *Powerful Sensitivity In Life.*

Let your mind still and your heart open. Close your eyes and focus.

Take five deep breaths. Visualise your body filled with the brightest sunlight. Let your heart shine and energise in this powerful light. See the heart energised and empowered in this golden sunlight. See the heart being held. You have the power to neutralise your sensitivity. BEING POWERFULLY IN YOUR LIGHT. Really connect with and energise this. You are firmly anchored in life. YOU ARE POWERFUL.

4. *Positive Life Directions.*

Let your heart and mind expand. Take five deep breaths.

Write down all the positive qualities that are powerfully you. Take one beautiful quality. Expand it in immense light. Connect with the quality. How can this quality flow and create a dynamic life direction. How can you utilise this quality to define who you are and express who you are in life. How can that quality touch others?

Take five deep breaths and see yourself being and expressing that quality in a life direction. YOU ARE POWERFUL AND IN THE FLOW.

5. Connect with archangel Raphael as name or symbol. Raphael is infinite healer. You can awaken the infinite healer within you. Powerfully yet gently healing and awakening you to the power of the infinite self and divine/universal healing energies.

6. Connect with archangel Michael by name or symbol. Awakening a deep vision of your life purpose. Archangel Michael activates powerful spiritual and psychological tools to expand consciousness beyond what we have experienced. Archangel Michael brings the ability to understand what is required for self awakening and the deepest healing on every level.

CHAPTER 19

LEARNING TO SOUL COACH YOURSELF

"I grew up in a safe and happy environment. My mother has always been the hub of the family, making sure we all sat down to family lunch on a Sunday and had lots of special family occasions, like birthday dinners to remember. We never had much money, but having twin brothers and a little sister we made our own entertainment.

I was born serious. My mother said that I was never an infant, but born an adult. This remains in my life now, since I often reflect on the more serious side of life and find it hard to lighten up. Whilst my brothers and sister were most often found playing or watching TV, I remember spending a lot of time in my bedroom alone, making little story books - always doing something quite crafty. I couldn't be bothered with toys. I liked quiet. And I found it hard to be around my loud cockney mother and boisterous brothers - even though I loved them dearly. As an adult I still hate noise especially confrontation and arguments - eating at these times is impossible.

I was very much a loner as a child and teenager. I could never really be bothered with kids in the playground, preferring my own company! I remember being extremely responsible and methodical, even as a young person. This held me in good stead for my career later. By the time I reached twenty-six my life was all that I wanted. After graduating from my degree in arts with a first class honours I immediately started a rapid and successful career path. I owned my own flat in London and had a great job as a creative director in media. Plus a great social life, clothes, holidays and money to spare.

I met my soulmate, now husband, on an aeroplane. We were both going to Thailand. After a shy and steady start, I very quickly realised that this was the person I wanted to be with. I instantly began to learn things I knew I needed to know from him, and I also felt there were things

I could offer this person in life. It was very much a love match, and was and continues to be a life affirming experience.

Everything in my life was in place, my partner, my home, work and friends. But something was not complete....Just a feeling. Some other energy I had not explored. Nothing drastic...I heard about Tracey Ash. I was particularly drawn to The College of Psychic Studies. This place was not a place labelled New Age. It seemed professional, which I was. So I signed up for a course with Tracey. At this point in my life the weekly sessions worked as a way to relax and re-focus my energy once a week. When else would I have the time or focus to sit, mediate and concentrate on my own energy? I did not have enough time in my fifty hour working week so at least one evening felt good - empowering. But I wanted more. Maybe at this point I wanted to start integrating my awareness.

Being pregnant made me work on myself - this was not just about Tracey working with my future direction but me looking at my own choices. She taught me meditations using positive energy leading up to the birth. I attended one anti-natal class of women concerned about how to deal with the birth - a room full of negativity. No thanks. Tracey encouraged me to concentrate on this child and the experience of having a child as part of my positive, life affirming soul purpose. After an easy and quick natural childbirth, Jackson was born.

After having Jackson I went back to weekly sessions and used them in a completely different way. My energy had changed, I was no longer strutting around an office in high heels, bossing around a bunch of crazy designers or going out most nights socialising. I was at home with my son, taking long walks, cooking and nurturing a young family. It was a rewarding and positive time. I was also very tired since Jackson was never good at sleeping and had bad colic. So the weekly classes were a great way to revitalise my energy; to learn how to quickly, in a matter of minutes, tap into the power of my own energy and feel aware. These sessions were healing and positive awakenings.

I see the work I have done with Tracey as learning how to life coach myself. Not therapy and not healing. To be in the moment. To feel alive. Not just for key moments in your life, like having a child, a partner, success in life - but in every moment.

Elizabeth

Liz is an incredibly powerful case study to consider. She shows great strength in focussing her individuality and authenticity in her life vision. Already with a successful career in media behind her, Liz felt there was still something else for her to discover. The Life Vision programme helped Liz to discover pioneering approaches to her life vision and what her work vision could be. This case study really does embrace a time of awakening - when worlds and ideas fuse. Liz could have trained as a fashion designer and worked in pure fashion but the work of the Life Vision programme inspired her to be more. Expansive energy and inspiration gave her the power base to not only become mum in the most soul conscious way but to also pioneer in a vibrant and new work vision - that focuses upon fashion in life-style. A progressive concept that would bring worlds together - of fashion, nutrition, make-up, styling, colour and life vision.

Liz was able to tap into the power of a successful career and fuse it with the most exquisite fashion pieces truly embracing who a woman is. Liz has taken the power of life vision training to develop sensitivity and intuition that can be used in women's lives. For all of us, it is a lesson in daring to be who we truly are - to dare to pioneer; to dare to step out of the perceived mould. I work with Liz. She is embarking upon a project that will take this business concept into the city for working women. Once again, she takes her power to initiate an innovative work vision that sits between worlds. She is daring all women to truly discover and express who they are.

Life Vision Affirmations

- I am unique

- I am powerful to hold my creative and professional vision

- I am powerful to hold home and work balance

- I can access energy, inspiration and the discipline to achieve and create my life vision

Life Vision Programme

1. *Knowing The Heart.*

Take five deep breaths. Sit comfortably. Close your eyes. Focus on the heart. Focus on opening your heart. Let the mind still. And let the heart and mind flow and connect as one. This is a powerful, vibrant connection that sparkles. This exercise allows you to truly communicate from the wisdom of your heart and mind.

Take five deep breaths. Ask the question: WHO AM I? Let your heart and mind explore.

Take five deep breaths and once more ask this question. WHO AM I? Draw or write what you sense and know. If you receive only a word be positive - this is a wonderful seed. You can go back into the exercise and start from this seed. Asking the same question: WHO AM I? Let your power and creativity flow as you tap into who you really are. CREATE AND EXPRESS WHO YOU TRULY ARE.

2. *Loving You.*

The power of loving you is important in your awakening. See or feel just how powerful your heart is - to energise, inspire and heal who you are. See the heart as vibrant, all powerful. See you alive in the power of your heart. See you alive and powerful in the activities you love doing, with the people you love and the places you love to connect with.

3. *My Life Vision.*

Write down your hopes and dreams for yourself. Write down your hopes and dreams as a child. What do really need to create in your life? Who do you need to connect with? You can also ask these questions after sitting comfortably and visualising you as powerful as the sun.

Take five deep breaths. Expand as the sun and open to your hopes and dreams.

4. *Work Vision.*

Write or draw the power qualities of you in work. Or the qualities you wish to create in work.

Take five deep breaths. Closing your eyes and sitting very comfortably, take one quality into each session. Expand into the power of the sun. Visualise or know that this quality is expanding within. See or recognise that this quality can expand beyond self into your work relationships. Into how you operate in a group. How you network or how you create work. Examples: COMMUNICATION, INTEGRITY, CREATIVITY,

5. *Work: Insight.*

Taking you to new levels of awareness and flow in your life. Sit comfortably and close your eyes. Take five deep breaths.

Clearing the heart and mind. Place a diamond of light in the heart and one in the mind. Take an avenue or direction in your life.

Take five deep breaths. Get a sense of the outcome. Of a flow or not? How does this feel? Does it sit well? If it does, let your power flow into it, connecting with it.

6. Connect with archangel Gabriel as name or symbol. Gabriel is the creator. Gabriel will awaken self love and the deepest authenticity. If you are already aware that facets of your life are empowering- deepen this

awareness by activating the deepest self and creative power. Gabriel will powerfully awaken you as a woman- to the divine feminine within. Gabriel will also powerfully activate creativity and creative vision especially in the way you create from the divine feminine and communicate this with others. Powerfully awakening Gabriel will expand the divine feminine in all that you do- through self, lifestyle, fashion, communication, spirituality and bring the potential to create deepest beauty and perfection in all that you do and create.

CHAPTER 20

TRACEY'S LIFE STORY

It is important that I include my life story.

"From a very early age I found my psychic sensitivity very difficult. I felt everything and everyone. I found being psychic very difficult to live with. Many generations of my family - my mother and grandmother - are naturally psychic. Both of my daughters are also very gifted psychically and this powerful gift has passed down through many generations including my cousins and their daughters.

As a child, there was conflict over accepting my psychic ability- my life purpose. My life has been full of learning, excitement, insight, healing and challenges. I have always relied upon my deep sense of knowing and the strength and ability to overcome whatever life challenges me with. From very early on, I have always known that my psychic gift was both powerful and healing. .

Since childhood, I have always been aware that I am a healer in the same way that I am today. I am a Life Visionary and Life Healer. The only difference is that at 36 years, I am more focused than ever into my Life Purpose. Since childhood I have always worked with life healing. I arrived knowing how to connect and work with soul in highly positive, empowering and multi-dimensional ways. I knew how to meditate without anyone in my family teaching me or even practicing. I regularly saw spirit and communicated with guides. I regularly tapped into how people felt. I regularly reached into future events. I arrived knowing how it worked! As a child I had highly developed psychic ability.

I was always aware of my natural abilities as healer who could easily access psychic information. When I was nine, for example, I recall being completely overwhelmed by a sense of need to care for and talk with a little girl in the school playground who had leukaemia. I knew that she would die and I felt her pain, her exclusion, the way that she had to put up with being bullied because she had no hair. I found that completely unacceptable. I made friends with her. I knew that I must. I have always been able to access how people feel. This I really took for granted. I assumed that everyone could do this.

I was born an Indigo in 1969 - possibly 20 years sooner than the many Indigo children born in recent decades. Indigo is a term developed by Jan Tober and Lee Carroll in their book Indigo Children. Indigos have a deep sense of purpose and many have an acute sense of awareness at a very young age. Indigos are groundbreaking for humanity in terms of the way humanity thinks, creates and communicates. They can also be very difficult and very misunderstood! I was accompanied by this new energy with powerful psychic and healing sensitivity and abilities. I felt every-thing. I was dis-empowered by my sensitivity- a very important facet of learning in my life journey. I had to learn to be dis-empowered first so crucial in awakening compassion for others. So crucial in expanding into empowered life vision. At that time there were far fewer Indigo children than today. Indigo has become such a popular term for a new generation of children born with very special gifts and very special energy. And it was really difficult being an Indigo kid in the 70s, especially in the 80s and certainly some of the 90s.

Being born an Indigo is the reason why my work today is pioneering. I see a new vision for healing, consciousness and information. One that fully embraces a modern spirituality in our modern world in new levels of insight and energy for living. My life journey as a result of this, has developed The Life Visionary and Life Healer that I have become. From earliest childhood, my life purpose was to understand whom I needed to help, whether it was a positive experience or not. Working with my psychic and healing abilities from very early on in my life was a very conscious soul contract for me. I instinctively knew who to help and for how long.

As a child, I found it all incredibly difficult to cope with. It was difficult to stay focused and I could get tired very easily. If I lost my focus I could open to too much psychic information and I sometimes felt like I was being lost in a sea of information. I could lose sight of myself around too many people. The possibility of downloading too much information brought sleeplessness, anxiety, fears and emotional see-sawing from childhood into my teens. I was ultra sensitive, being able to connect with and, importantly, transform other people's emotions and moods. I could record and download everything from how someone was feeling, to the way they walked, talked and thought. I didn't have to make any effort - I could just do it. I never really wanted this to happen. At times it left me emotionally exhausted and physically drained.

One of my earliest psychic experiences occurred when I was about five years old. I recall not being able to sleep well and always being highly sensitive at night. I woke one night to see a beautiful pale blue/grey woman dressed in nineteenth century clothing. She stood silently and peacefully watching over me. I know now that she is one of my spirit teachers but then, I did not understand. I opened my mouth and froze- no words could or would come out. I hid under the blankets still sensing that she was watching over me. I managed a, "Maaa, Maaam." "Why me I?" I thought, "Why watch over me?" I looked again and she was still there!

My greatest joy as a young child came in morning when the sun filled my room and I could watch the orbs of light dancing in front of me. Early on, I recognised my ability to communicate with unseen dimensions. I thought a lot about universes within universes. I was also particularly sensitive to emotions feeling anger in people would cause me to freeze and lose my voice. Being psychic could make life quite difficult. As a ten year old I remember being ill and absent from school. I recall knowing that when I returned to school, my best friend would no longer be my best friend and I that I would be no longer be sitting next to her. It all happened just as I had accessed. She had indeed acquired a new best friend who would be her best friend.

As a child I was forever talking with my mother about what I saw or had connected with. She constantly tried to reinforce that it was my imagination. She was secretly hoping that I might skip being so psychically sensitive - obviously that wasn't going to happen. My upbringing was very traditional in many ways. I grew up in middle class, suburban Newcastle Upon Tyne. My father worked hard to give us the life he had never had. He came from a proud working class background and worked in construction.. My mother is a housewife with crippling arthritis. She is a natural healer and medium. Now in her late fifties, she has spent much of her life caring for people who are dying. Her life has worked with people with cancer and learning to know other people's pain - physical and emotional - in their journeys towards their deaths. Her physical health has been very damaged as a result of decades of healing others. By her late fifties my mother has suffered multiple strokes.

Very male and female roles dominated our household and our childhood but a magical and matriarchal grandmother played a key role in helping me to understand my psychic gifts.

My Nana, as I called her, was the oldest of eleven children. She worked hard but had an avid interest in mediumship. She and my grandfather attended séances and mediumship demonstrations during the war. Some people say that you can always tell that a person is a psychic or medium by their eyes and in my family this is so true - the cool, pale, blue eyes have been passed to each generation of naturally gifted psychics and healers. There is a depth and wisdom beyond the years. In my family - it appears to arise eldest daughter to eldest daughter. It can indicate a life to be lived to the full, a life of challenges and learning about deep personal pain and life beyond death.

My grandmother was a very realistic, hardworking woman whose life was not consumed by searching for proof of her psychic experiences. She merely accepted her gifts as a very natural part of her being. She had very real and direct experiences of spirit, having very natural mediumistic abilities that passed to my mother, then to me and my daughters. Eventually, after her death, she came to be one of my spirit helpers.

This story will help you to place my mother and grandmother within my life story. In 1967, my uncle Tommy's wife, Doreen, died. She was in her late twenties. My aunt died close to midnight from a heart attack and there was nothing my uncle could do for her; she died in his arms before the doctor could get to her. At that time, my mother was still living at home. On the night my aunt died, she and my grandmother both heard footsteps running up the stairs to their flat. It was midnight.

They opened the door but no one was there – this was the very moment that my aunt had died

When I was a teenager, I had a dream about my grandmother that would have a profound affect on my future direction. In the dream, I was told that my grandmother would die in six weeks. The information gave me the exact future date, the place and circumstances of her death- in hospital with all her family around her – able to say goodbye to everyone she loved when she died. I told some friends about my dream, that I knew gran would be dying soon. Almost six weeks later, my grandmother's radiant health went into rapid and unsuspected decline and within two days she was rushed into hospital. I managed to get most of her close family to her bed before she died and I was relieved that most of them could make it. Even though the scenario was deeply disturbing, I recognised my psychic gift as being a very positive in my life. I also recognised that the information was astonishingly accurate and very uncomfortable for others to deal with. I thought that it was so natural but my friends and family found it difficult to accept.

Nana's death earmarked the passing of her spirit in a very peculiar way. Although her death was sudden and her physical illness made her weak that she could not walk, in her last moments she sat up and stood up to walk. She spoke directly to her deceased brothers at the end of the bed. Calling them by each of their names. I remember her saying that she just wasn't in anyway ready to go and leave us. She almost argued her point.

Around that time, I also realised that living with my psychic ability was becoming more difficult. My Gran's spirit was with me for several weeks after her death. In fact, during her funeral wake, several pieces of glassware were thrown off my mother's tall display cabinet, although no one had touched the cabinet. The glassware fell a metre and a half but did not smash - it stayed perfectly intact. Her funeral guests were terrified. "Its good, old Gran", I joked, "She was always stubborn." It was her sheer determination to send proof that caused the glassware to fall but not shatter. Gran had proved her point - life after death. It made me laugh; it made her funeral guests pale and make for a quick exit to the pub. But it wasn't only the mediumship or connecting with her spirit that really interested me. It was also the dream and the quality of the psychic information that made me decide, at 18, that I would eventually become a psychic.

Creative Vision

In Newcastle, there is an unspoken language - living from intuition and humour- always thinking and joking ahead. My Dad's mother defied tradition to marry for love. She ran away from her catholic family and turned her back on a wealthy life to marry my grandfather, who was very poor. I have probably inherited some of that stubbornness from Grandmother Ash - to defy the traditional. In the twenties, she challenged her family and all ties with her were severed. She went against the grain to be with the man she loved, had eleven children, and lived happily without much money to spare. I am very fortunate to have roots in families with such strong women.

As a child and teenager, however, I was determined not to carry on the strong, matriarchal role where women's lives focus and revolve almost solely around the family. It felt so outdated. Both my brother and I were loved and totally supported to live our dreams but my mother expected that I would follow her and live in Newcastle. This vision was difficult for her to give up although I had decided early on that my pathway would be creative and academic. This was partly so that my psychic sensitivity could be balanced.

I planned at an early age to leave Newcastle to do this. I had developed a love for the challenge of creativity and inspiration in the arts and could work with my intuition and psychic abilities in fine art and design. I did my A levels and focused on going to art college. I had developed a love for art from the age of thirteen years old. Creating art was a sacred space purely for me. It gave me space and time away from channelling psychic information for other people. Art college was a direct link into using my intuition and inspiration. Fine art was a love and passion of mine but I chose fashion design instead. Interestingly, using and developing psychic abilities is key as you design seasons ahead. At art college, I developed visual skills - the ability to see and conceptualise in the mind. I developed strong psychic abilities through art in fashion prediction.

But by the end of the course, in 2003, I knew that working in this way was not enough for me. I felt strongly that I should be working with people on a much deeper level. In the previous year I had had a near death experience and it had blown me wide open psychically. It was a gift in itself. It was showing me the way back into working as a pure channel and psychic and would lead me to working with people on much deeper soul and healing levels. It happened in a car while I was out with some people I thought I knew whilst in the summer recess from art college, and I was drugged.. Divine intervention luckily brought road works and I managed to escape from the car and the people who had done this to me. I was seriously ill and a family called an ambulance for me. I remember feeling myself slipping in and out of consciousness.

The outcome brought my own near death experience at hospital and an encounter with my grandmother's spirit. She told me that she was with me and I would not die. As the paramedics worked on me, I felt the overwhelming physical presence of my grandmother healing me. I had faced death. My psychic sensitivity was now so open that I knew that my life would be changing radically. I also knew that my psychic abilities had to be harnessed. I could now tap into everything so much more acutely than before. I had to focus upon awakening my life purpose as a tool for healing and controlling my psychic abilities.

My life purpose was clear- psychic and healer. Indeed, the near death experience catapulted my psychic abilities so much that I could no longer brush them aside and drew me further away from fashion design. A year later, in my final year, just before finishing art college, I met a soul mate, Jorge, who had a deep impression upon my life and my need for spirituality. His interest in ecology and the world accelerated my need to do more in the world. He was a very calming influence in my life. He was focused on, and working towards, studying in the UK.

Our coming together really helped us both to discover just what we were both capable of achieving in our lives. I have never met before or since anyone so deeply spiritual and unaffected by it. He showed and taught me this in his complete honesty and integrity when dealing with people. He always retained an ability to remain true to himself in all kinds of situations and with whomever he came into contact. He had a stillness that only meditation can bring although I never saw him meditate in the five years we were together. When I discovered The College of Psychic Studies, he encouraged me to go there. We parted at the end of five years - we were always very clear that he had no interest in developing spiritually and psychically. He didn't need to do this.

He was a beautiful, spiritual teacher who taught me a deep sense of spirituality and knowing just what that is. I was a soul mate in his life who helped him to make the transition to living and studying ecology in the UK. We loved each other but our contracts were designed to help each other at very difficult times in our lives. We both understood when it was time to leave the relationship. The last time I spoke with Jorge, he was getting married and I was pregnant with my first daughter. We were both happy for each other - our contracts were over - we could let each other go.

The College of Psychic Studies, London

I knew instinctively that The College of Psychic Studies was the only place for me to study. This was the mid 90's and I was 23. I immediately fell in love with the challenge to develop precise and intelligent approaches as a psychic communicator.

The College of Psychic Studies dates back to 1884, leads worldwide in psychic and healing professional training and is an outstanding centre for exploration of consciousness. I remember my first class at The College of Psychic Studies, I awakened. I was home. I knew that this was where I belonged and that this work was going to be my empowered life purpose from now on. I felt so alive. I knew that I could now live with and develop my psychic sensitivity to its full potential.

I recall being a student at The College of Psychic Studies in a development class of a very gifted trance medium, Richard Ward-Roden, in the 90s. It was then that I truly understood that it was the right time - that I would be a psychic so that I could help others. This is one of the fundamental reasons why I work with clients today. My purpose in this field is as a channel, healer, teacher and investigator. I am driven by a fascination to investigate information as an intelligent tool to heal, transform and understand life. From early in life and throughout my psychic training, I recognised a deep inner need to bring these concepts to others. I also recognised my purpose to bring this work to the modern world- to people who would not normally access psychic information.

I began building the bridge between conventional and unconventional worlds. Working as a professional, I began to recognise my acute abilities to break down the mechanics and techniques of psychic information, not purely for information but to bring a deeper understanding of self to my clients. In Life Vision sessions I was able to access information on life purpose and life vision. My Life Vision sessions accelerated and developed at such a speed to combine information with massive transformation and healing. The life purpose information positively affects my clients so that life changes can take place. Still today, I am learning how to do this more powerfully, more precisely, to awaken life vision into powerful new world vision. I am fascinated continuously. In every moment I strive for excellence.

As I explored my own advanced psychic and healing approaches in life vision sessions, I discovered I could discipline my focus to travel into specific levels for my clients when asked. Being able to navigate the client's life vision matrix meant total precision. The client identifies with information on all levels- particularly a unique Life Vision in the modern world. The Life Vision session gives a framework of information and the life power tools to activate Life Vision in the most powerful and inspirational way. It gives the client a way to find a modern spirituality whether it is through creativity or teaching, or living in the country or being a mother. Your role and purpose in modern life becomes everything and everyone that resonates with you and inspires you. It identifies who you are and why you are who you are. It develops who you are and your life vision.

Soul Connections

I have so many connections with my husband, a continuity and eternity that bonds us together in this life. As a child, on my first visit to London aged ten years, I knew that, as an adult, I would live in London and I was immediately drawn to St James' Church, Piccadilly. I knew then, it would be an important place in my life and indeed, it was here that I met my husband in 1997 almost twenty years on.

There was an immediate connection and recognition. I knew it; he knew it. Our existing relationships were almost over. By the time I was twenty five, I also knew that Martin was the name of my husband to be. We did nothing about this connection for months. I knew that I wanted to be ready for this relationship. We both waited and in the spring, he kept asking me to date him.

This soulmate relationship is a complex one. Martin is sixteen years older than me with two marriages behind him. I knew that this soulmate relationship was going to be difficult. I knew this would be a magical and spiritually exciting relationship - of deep emotional and psychological discussion that would be a huge learning ground for both of us. I knew this soulmate relationship would teach us about love and loving. I also knew that I was absolutely terrified of how powerful this relationship was going to be. We would be drawn together and almost torn apart.

My husband has played a key role in helping to shape the person I am today and awakening me fully into my life purpose. He has guided me, intellectually challenged and expanded my psychic development through his ability to analyse. This has taught me, too, how to demonstrate the validity and intelligence of the work that I do today. He has also helped me to develop an unshakable interest in the psychic and psychological so that I can work with a modern approach to psychic channelling.

He has always challenged and questioned my work and this has helped me develop as a powerful, creative channel, teacher and writer. He accelerates these gifts in me. He has made the transition from artist to training as counsellor. We have both supported our respective life visions. We have two incredibly spirited daughters who reinforce who we are and what we need to become.

This is not the perfect love story, however. Martin had ties to the past that we needed to free ourselves from in order for our relationship to work. There were issues and old energy from one of his past relationships that we would have to face in our future together. In the early stages of our relationship we got around to talking about my birthday. The conversation went something like this:

"I used to live here - just up here. This was my first house," Martin said. It was a cottage in Richmond.

"Oh," I said, thinking that I didn't really need to know where he had lived with his first wife.

"So," he said, "when is your birthday?

"Twenty fifth November."

"What? Twenty fifth November? That is the birthday of my second wife," he said.

I could sense him feeling very uneasy and disconnecting from me as we drove up the road. The coincidence was uncanny but more followed. Not only did I share the same birthday date with his second wife (with whom I have had no connection) but his first wife's surname was Tracey. The karmic ties and significance of this relationship took several years to unfold.

Martin's first wife, Wilma, was diagnosed with cancer very early on in our relationship. I was in love. I didn't think about Wilma at that time. She was in France with Martin's daughter. In the spring that we started dating and she was diagnosed with cancer, Martin's divorce from his second wife was proceeding. I am a very strong and practical person - but from the very start of our relationship there would be interference from his first wife, Wilma. She wanted him back. And for a person like Wilma it would be a fight until the end.

During the subsequent years, I learned how incredibly hard it was for Wilma to let Martin go. She didn't necessarily want him, but she couldn't let him go either - and her cancer was part of that letting go. I gradually understood that I had to face a very powerful woman who thought that she could never lose to anything or anyone. She was strong psychically and psychologically. Everyone she came into contact with she controlled. This would be key to me really acknowledging my own power. In our first meeting, I became incredibly aware of who she really was. I wouldn't be controlled. I have never felt such an overwhelming feeling of knowing that someone was so wrong for me to be around. I felt her pain and anger that she was using to control everyone.

My intuition warned that I would have to keep my distance from Wilma. This was key to unlocking her control over Martin. I knew that if

I was to help Martin and honour our relationship, I would have to prove my own power and integrity to deal her. It was like meeting someone worlds apart. There was no meeting place for this woman. Her world was on her terms only. Wilma took an immediate dislike to me for the simple reason that I was everything that she was not. I would be teaching her that she could not control everything including me. She, in turn, would be teaching about my power. Our learning was to understand our vision of our own power in our lives - even learning to respect our very different visions and to honour that. Wilma was another person who has accelerated my psychic potential and gifts. I was faced with really honouring my power and who I am.

The situation with Wilma was also key in helping me understanding my soul group connections. I knew that I was involved with Martin to help him end her control. Her need to control and hold onto him had a strong and negative energetic connection. He told me that he had been asleep for eight years from the day he had met Wilma. When he woke up, it took him another four years to leave her. Martin needed to totally free himself of this past. This would come later.

Sometimes in our lives we meet life accelerators and he is one of those soulmates who perfects my every flaw. Being with Martin brought rapid spiritual and psychic growth. We work on every aspect of each other, every connection between us is supported and connected to bring positive flow- however difficult. He supported my transition from designer to life visionary and teacher. He has helped me to build and develop my work so that I work from a place of integrity and heart to work with others.

The first twelve months of our relationship was massively healing and revealed our healing issues, our deepest fears and insecurities. Here was the challenge - nothing could be hidden because we knew each other already too well. We never stopped talking and discussing from the day we met. At the same time, Martin's first wife, Wilma, appeared back in the picture. She moved back to London with Ruby, desperate to get back with Martin once she heard that his divorce from his second wife was imminent.

Martin was clear that he did not want her. However, her presence and negativity could be felt at a great distance. I recall an exhibition that Martin had organised early on in our relationship, that she and her friends were not invited to. I felt her immense anger about not being invited the night before the exhibition, as did Martin. We weren't even staying together on that night. I was in south London and Martin was in Ealing. I intuited early on that we had to be firm about not letting this woman into our lives. It would prove to be far more difficult than I anticipated.

By July 2001, Wilma's cancer had returned and spread into her liver. She continued to battle on with work and avoided looking at the root cause of her cancer, which she needed to do in order to start healing herself. She would not be helped. I suggested counselling. She refused. She just did not connect with the concept of healing, nor did she understand that she had the major role in her own healing. Healing could not be paid for or left to others to do for her. Perhaps she did not believe in her power to heal herself but what I did understand was that this woman was disintegrating because of her need to control. A vast lesson for anyone to learn - one many of us face in different ways in our lives - but an especially painful lesson when you are leaving a young daughter behind. Her daughter was only ten years old and as a mother, I could connect with her agony - leaving her child behind. Even my empathy she used against me. What I would never understand, though, were her reasons for hatred especially towards my children.

At that time, this woman's late father contacted me in spirit. He gave me his name, Tommy. He indicated his concern for her health and that she was dying. It felt crazy at the time that this man was contacting me. He indicated that she would die around a wedding and kept referring to a wedding. Two years later - three weeks after our wedding - she died. He was absolutely right! His reference to a wedding had not made sense at the time as Martin and I had not decided yet to get married; our decision came almost eighteen months after Tommy communicated with me.

I was working at The College of Psychic Studies when Wilma died. I felt her spirit rush towards me and a plant fell from the mantel. I knew that she was gone. Ruby, her daughter, came to live with us but that wasn't the end of the story. Back in 2001, Wilma created a family settlement that handed over all power of her estate to trustees for eighty years. She first refused to co-operate in any way with us to make practical financial plans for the time of her death. She would not co-operate but tried to force her control onto our family way past her death. This was most apparent in the way she tried to manipulate my family to move back to London by the terms laid down in the family settlement. There was no consideration at all for my family and especially my children.

Wilma left a legacy that didn't consider the changes that would have to be made for Ruby coming to live with us. Over the next few years, the outcome of her strict legacy and instructions would make it as difficult as possible for Ruby to settle with us and for me to be her new mother. Martin had let the legacy in and it would take several years to disconnect with it.

At the same time, our youngest daughter, India, was diagnosed with Neurofibromatosis. I was devastated. Only a few months after our wedding, our family was falling apart. There was so much to deal with and Martin and I did not have the time to talk. Martin's business nosedived so I was having to work longer hours to support the family. In addition to Ruby's grief and India's genetic condition, there was no time for us to connect with each other. I was exhausted and India's condition became paramount . I needed space to be practical about this. India was facing possible learning difficulties, dyspraxia and dyslexia. Symptoms of this condition sometimes don't show until a child is in her teens.

I decided that the girls and myself really needed some space, especially in dealing with India's condition. Martin had given Ruby India's room. I took the train and left. Martin at this time was emotionally vulnerable to only thinking about Ruby. He made agreements with the

Trust to move out of our family home and rent a property until Ruby would be eighteen. With Ruby in private education the trustees had achieved their goal. I was devastated to hear that our family home had been swept aside.

We were both also fighting freedom from Wilma's control and, as I look back to that time, I realise that we were both fighting each other in order to free our family. We both had to grow incredibly strong spiritually to deal with what was to happen. We almost lost our relationship. We were learning about love in the harshest way but we had to remain apart to see each other clearly. I returned after three months..

In the eighteen months from Wilma's death, there was so much inter-ference from her friends through the Trust that Wilma had set up. The bitterness ran deep. One of the trustees thought he was Ruby's father. He had been manipulated too. I knew and felt strongly that these people had no part in our lives. They feigned concern for Ruby but their intention was to create a divide in our family. In the final meeting that we had with the trustees, their manipulation and need for revenge was made clear. We had been openly honest about our situation both emotionally and practically and in our need for a larger home for our family to support all our children, including Ruby. They refused to give us any practical support and, in that final meeting, it all became clear.

All I could feel in that meeting was my unshakable love for my husband and family and the realisation that these people were out to control all of us, including all three children. During the meeting, every-thing slowed for me. My anger smoothed as I realised my children would never be controlled. I could feel my love for my family and myself. It lifted me away from the negativity so that I could see the situation for all that it was. I knew we had no need to allow these people in our lives and, two days later, we cut off all connections with them. The control is gone. We are all free – but especially my girls, to live their lives without restrictions and control. Ruby, as she gets older, will have to deal with this legacy and the possibility of never inheriting her estate without control and manipulation.

It felt like everyone on both sides had been drawn into a web that Wilma had created. We decided to tell Ruby everything. We moved out of the rented house. The universe confirmed our freedom eight months later we bought a beautiful family home. The freedom I sought for my family brought a freedom in my life purpose to support exactly what we needed as a family. Time and time again, it takes me back to my authenticity.

Our Daughters

Our daughter, Scarlett, decided upon Martin and I to be her parents. This is my account of her journey in to the physical, accompanied by the spirit of Martin's father who I had not met at anytime before his death. What is amazing is that Scarlett was present around me six months before her conception with the spirit of Martin's father. The story demonstrates my gift to key into what we don't see everyday. It draws upon the magic of conception and birth. Unseen dimensions and information, including communication with my daughter to be with her grandfather in spirit. The account demonstrates what I hold so very dear to my heart. This knowledge I bring to my work - my spiritual learning of love, parenthood and a soul's conception. I was aware of a spirit child around me six months before Scarlett was conceived and I told Martin that we would be parents. He was doubtful and very afraid. Our relationship had just really begun - we had not even thought about being together on such a permanent basis.

When I had met Martin six months earlier in 1998, the timing perfect - we had both left relationships of five years behind us and both needed some space and time to come into this relationship. I knew that he would be my husband immediately. We had to learn to trust and love each other. I don't think either of us reckoned on our child coming so soon but Scarlett had other ideas.

Scarlett appeared first as a spirit child in Richard Ward-Roden's class at The College of Psychic Studies. I was not yet pregnant. I began seeing this bright spirit child. She circled me and made it quite clear that we belonged together. Any mother knows that connecting with her child is a miracle in itself. The miracle for me was in the way we did it before conception and all during pregnancy. It was one of the most incredible connections with communicating with spirit - my beloved daughter, yet to be conceived. It was wonderful to be so aware. As a mother I could work with the soul of my child - a pre-birth soul connection. This profound experience was born out of our souls really needing to experience each other- and loving her - and drawing her with ease into the physical dimension. I even heard her cry before her birth.

Interestingly, Martin's father had died several years before Martin and I had met. His father appeared in spirit to me and gave me his name, Bobby, which Martin confirmed. As a medium, I found it fascinating that Scarlett was accompanied by her grandfather's spirit. Martin's father helped bring Scarlett into the physical. His father was also supporting our relationship. Martin refused to accept what I had accessed. His father had left him when he was one and moved to Australia. In that time he had seen him once. However, the child and grandfather continued to be present on many occasions at home, at The College of Psychic Studies, at Martin's flat even in restaurants. This was no case of isolated communication. His father clearly expressed that he was so sorry that he had left Martin as a child for Australia. He did this so powerfully one night that he spoke through Martin. His contract was to bring Scarlett to us and help bring us together. He would put his mistake right. He would also play a major role in dealing with Wilma.

In August 1999, we went to France and headed for Carnac for the solar eclipse. Martin's father appeared with Scarlett in France. When we returned to London, I discovered that I was four months pregnant. The communication I had with my child and her grandfather was astonishing.

The miracle of parenting and understanding it from unseen dimensions left me truly open to love and understand the spiritual cycle of life. What a pre-pregnancy! What a pregnancy! Scarlett and her grandfather awakened my awareness to the spiritual process of creation- how a soul connects enters the world. I can never forget just how profound connecting with Scarlett has been.

My pregnancy with Scarlett was so beautiful- a spiritual awakening and understanding for me throughout. She opened my insight into other worlds. Her birth was sacred. Although in pain, I was aware of Martin's father, my grandmother and White Feather- my guide assisting this beautiful soul – Scarlett Grace. Her birth was silent, sacred, deeply amazing - it blew my mind. She arrived as perfection. I recognised an old, old soul incredibly at ease with the world. She was tranquil, calm and wise. She opened her eyes and looked at each one of us. The medical team left us. I cried. She did not look as though she had endured the trauma of birth at all. She arrived with a timeless beauty and intelligence that she still retains as a four year old. She has taught me what love, stillness, maturity, truth, integrity and creativity are.

As soon as Scarlett had arrived, I knew that I would be pregnant again very soon. I was very aware of our conscious choice. Pregnancy beckoned two month's later. By this time, we had moved out of London. My second daughter, India, certainly did not present herself in the same way as Scarlett.

In fact, India didn't really arrive into her physical body until after three hours after her birth. The birth itself was incredible - a fascinating experience that embraced working consciously with spirit. India was almost born in the hospital lobby - she was that close. There was little time to think about connecting into the sacred space at childbirth – we had only just managed to get to hospital! Boy, was I just a little scared to give birth without pain relief! I panicked and breathed. As I breathed, I felt my connection with White Feather, my guide, who was also present for Scarlett's birth. I had an out of body experience. I was lifted out from my body as India born. India had been a little distressed and required a quick birth. As I showered afterwards, I was amazed at what had happened - a totally pain-free birth- I was aware but my awareness was outside of myself. The power of spirit, of White Feather, had intervened to support the birth of India.

India's soul didn't enter her body until three hours later when I was witness to the most beautiful and powerful child arriving. Her soul was being downloaded and I could see and sense the most intrinsic matrixes of energies and soul information entering her body. India represented the shift required in my insight and psychic abilities and she would challenge me to understand her. My traditional mediumistic abilities were now rendered useless. India required me to work with her soul on an entirely different level. I knew immediately that this child would be a very special teacher to me so that I could work on a more profound level with her and only then with others.

Certainly India Mae is not an Indigo child, as Scarlett and I are, although she is ultra-sensitive. The consequence of which made living in the physical a very immediate issue and problem for us to solve and overcome. She showed immediate sensitivity even to my breast milk in her first hours. She showed sensitivity to people and hardly slept at all. I was the only person who could soothe her. Even today, we are the closest of soul mates. Even today she is a powerful bridge between two worlds. She is an incredible healer.

As a psychic I knew that I had to develop new ways of working in order to help understand her. I also had to understand our soul contracts in order to work with and to heal her. What became very evident was that she responded really well to my healing and insight. Slowly, she started to de-sensitise to the environment and to other people. She began to sleep for longer periods and put on weight. However, that was not our only problem to face. At twelve months old, a follow-up check at the hospital with a dermatologist began to uncover a genetic condition called neurofibromatosis 1. This is linked to benign tumours that can develop through the nerve endings anywhere in the body. It appeared that India was showing signs of the condition on her body but the doctors weren't sure for nearly two years.

Both Martin and I were devastated by the implications of the condition because traditional orthodox medicine cannot treat this, apart from cutting the tumours out if they become too problematic. India was being faced with other possible future outcomes, too, including learning difficulties, ADD, behavioural problems, dyspraxia and dyslexia. She was totally embodying being an Indigo Child.

I began to use my immense psychic and healing resources to channel our soul contracts and to heal and work with India to empower and reinforce her energy field. I accessed information within her soul matrix over many months to activate flow and balance within her energy field. I searched specifically into my soul contracts with her. I tracked past life issues to identify any residual energies affecting her in this life. I checked and re-checked her sensitivity to environmental effects. I realised that our soul contracts demanded a shift in my consciousness, energy and awareness so that I could access information and higher healing relevant to understanding and healing India. She has completely directed the way that I channel today. She has been the major inspiration to all my work on Life Vision. My work for Indigo Children that has been filmed for My Child's Psychic, Cutting Edge, Channel Four.

As any parent will understand. You will do anything in your power to heal your child. Conventional medicine does not fully support India. I had to use my gifts for her. I accessed her soul information, so that I could understand what she required to heal herself. I immediately committed to a programme of support and healing for India. Every level was investigated. Every possible issue that was affecting her well-being was checked. I discovered that her sleeping problems were being caused by geopathic stress associated with the home we were living in so I immediately moved her into our room.

We sourced organic food and cleaning products to re-balance her sensitivities. She required intensive grounding and re-balancing through her whole energy field and central nervous system. I worked with Archangel healing, with Uriel, Michael, Raphael and Gabriel to heal her at one of the highest and safest healing levels. Channelled archangel healing work informed me how I needed to work with India. It did not over energise her - it centred her, it balanced her and it grounded her. I was amazed at the results. High level healing work could assist her connection to the world - she responded so immediately to channelled archangel healing. Our dear child began to connect more powerfully and vibrantly to the world.

The Awakening System became an intensive programme of healing and understanding for India. In accessing and healing her soul, I recognised how anchored she could become. This suggested that I could powerfully connect her body and soul. Over time and alongside this programme, India's digestive sensitivity reduced. Her confidence grew and her acute sensitivity to people has disappeared. Her voice, her energy, her personality are bold. Her prognosis is mild NF1 and she shows no signs of learning difficulties. Without India, my professional work would not have developed as it has.

My important aim with India is to develop my work with her so that I can assist her. As a five year old, she definitely knows that she is working with me. When she was three years old, in a children's workshop, I led the group and channelled Archangel Michael. In these workshops, children of two to fourteen years are taught how to meditate. We worked immediately into art and sculpture. India sat very quietly, " I am working with my mummy," she said. And she went on to paint what she had experienced in the meditation. She really experienced Archangel Michael as I had and other healers in the group. One of them commented upon India's focus, artwork and the way that she was really working with mummy that day. She painted magnificent columns of lavender and blue energy. It was subtle and beautiful - years beyond her age. She certainly communicates beyond her years! I really appreciate how much of a teacher she is to me.

The work with India has also translated into working with parents and children- so that parents can understand and heal their children. Highly advanced soul information and healing techniques of the highest levels have arisen from working with India. She has directed and developed Life Vision and The Awakening System with me. She has defined the use of multi-dimensional channelling in our lives and in my work. I am also well aware that she can remain well with the healing and insight she receives. I fully trust that her condition is now workable. This work with India is continuous.

CHAPTER 21

BALANCING OUR LIVES

" For the soul walks not upon a line, neither does it grow like a reed.
The soul unfolds itself, like a lotus of countless petals"
The Prophet, Kahil Gibran, 1922

For almost everyone, there will always be essential considerations in modern life over vital work-life balance. It applies to us all. There is always constant adjustment and awareness of the need for life flexibility that directs the way you learn about who you are and your life vision. Even if you do not consciously seek Life Vision we all learn through the challenges and breakthroughs of life. The demands of our lives and our journey of awakening are powerful anchors in modern life. No matter what your belief system is, there is a quest to always understand self and the world. One of love and healing. We are very much waking to the way we can discover self and the world, discover time and new energy to allow us to achieve more. Attitudes towards managing time and our energy is changing the quality of modern living.

I have always indicated that 2007 would be the key year of awakening and new world vision. I trust implicitly the communication I receive. With every life vision session this is reinforced. What has perhaps been arduous self and world realisation of an old world vision- is now majestically awakening a new world vision - new energy - new insight. As people awaken to life purpose as the core, driving force- awakening and healing who they truly are. It takes us into powerful authenticity. Only authenticity. And only authenticity for the world. It is a huge leap forward for consciousness in this new age - not only for self but an authentic connection and contribution to the world. Conscious creation and conscious healing is key to this new world vision that connects all.

My wish is that you find something in this book, no matter how small, in the case studies gifted by my clients or in the life vision techniques. I wish you an incredible journey of self-discovery, energy transformation and creation so that you can master and expand your life vision into the modern world. If you crave stillness, don't *think* about it, *access* it. If you *crave* inspiration, *create* the space to achieve it. We are entering a time like no other before when we can experience an awakening and mastery of consciousness - of just what can be achieved in the world. Our thoughts will be very quickly manifest in the modern world. We then, have to be authentic in all we create. It starts with self-discovery and the divine power of new insight and understanding. What this book hopes to awaken within you is the visionary, the creator, the alchemist and the infinite healer. Yet with this- awakening powerful life vision tools that can be used in the modern world.

Questions I leave you with: Where is your inspiration to awaken and transform self and the world? Where is your precision focus? Dare to step out of *I can't* and *I won't*. Inspire your life purpose and life vision and you will truly create an empowering new world vision.

It is an important time for us to explore and expand the very nature of who we are; to reach into depths of polarities that will awaken in all of us a very authentic power. Who we are is expanding and is being challenged by old limitations we have set for self and the world. We no longer require this limiting perspective of self and the world. This is the *limited I*. This exploration of polarities of right and wrong, authenticity and integrity, truth and non-truth is exciting and yet can be completely exhausting. It will bring us to a pivotal point in consciousness- *our awakening*. When we find authenticity and divinity within we can powerfully radiate true self, activating who we are in expanding life vision. This is the *infinite I*. This is modern spirituality- a quest of self discovery and new world vision awakening. The only way forward is BEING exactly who you are and living your authentic life vision.

Conscious healing

Conscious creation.

BIBLIOGRAPHY

Bailey, Alice- *The Rays and Initiations* Lucis Press Ltd, London, 1960

Bailey, Alice- *Telepathy* Lucis Press Ltd, London, 1950

Braden, Gregg- *The God Code* Hay House, 2004

Carrol, Lee and Tober, Jan- *Indigo Children* Hay House, 1999

Gibran, Kahil- *The Prophet* Penguin Books, 1923

Gribbon, John- *Star Dust The Cosmic Recycling of Stars, Planets and People* Allen Lane The Penguin Press, 2000

McTaggart, Lynn- *The Field* HarpersCollinsPublishers, 2003

Myss, Caroline- *Anatomy of the Spirit The Seven Stages of Power and Healing* Bantam, 1997

ABOUT THE AUTHOR

Tracey Ash and The Awakening System Programme has featured in the national press and Cutting Edge, Channel Four, My Child's Psychic. She has her own school The Awakening System in London and Bedfordshire. She is an expert in locating empowered life purpose and life vision for clients worldwide.

Tracey Ash is a channel, life visionary and life healer offering Life Purpose and Life Vision sessions worldwide.

The Awakening System Programme offers intensive training programmes in life vision, life purpose, the matrix, channelling, archangels, professional channelling and The Esoteric School.

She teaches, lectures and offers Life Vision sessions at The College of Psychic Studies, London.

For further information on The Awakening System Programme in UK and Corfu please contact www.theawakeningsystem.co.uk

BOOKS

O books

O is a symbol of the world, of oneness and unity. In different cultures it also means the "eye", symbolizing knowledge and insight, and in Old English it means "place of love or home". O books explores the many paths of understanding which different traditions have developed down the ages, particularly those today that express respect for the planet and all of life.

For more information on the full list of over 300 titles please visit our website
www.O-books.net

myspiritradio is an exciting web, internet, podcast and mobile phone global broadcast network for all those interested in teaching and learning in the fields of body, mind, spirit and self development. Listeners can hear the show online via computer or mobile phone, and even download their favourite shows to listen to on MP3 players whilst driving, working, or relaxing.

Feed your mind, change your life with O Books, The O Books radio programme carries interviews with most authors, sharing their wisdom on

life, the universe and everything...e mail questions and co-create the show with O Books and myspiritradio.

Just visit **www.myspiritradio.com** for more information.

Back to the Truth
5,000 years of Advaita
Dennis Waite

A wonderful book. Encyclopedic in nature, and destined to become a classic. **James Braha**

Absolutely brilliant...an ease of writing with a water-tight argument outlining the great universal truths. This book will become a modern classic. A milestone in the history of Advaita. **Paula Marvelly**
1905047614 500pp **£19.95 $29.95**

Beyond Photography
Encounters with orbs, angels and mysterious light forms
Katie Hall and John Pickering

The authors invite you to join them on a fascinating quest; a voyage of discovery into the nature of a phenomenon, manifestations of which are shown as being historical and global as well as contemporary and intently personal.

At journey's end you may find yourself a believer, a doubter or simply an intrigued wonderer... Whatever the outcome, the process of journeying is likely prove provocative and stimulating and - as with the mysterious images fleetingly captured by the authors' cameras - inspiring and potentially enlightening. **Brian Sibley**, author and broadcaster.
1905047908 272pp 50 b/w photos +8pp colour insert **£12.99 $24.95**

Don't Get MAD Get Wise

Why no one ever makes you angry, ever!

Mike George

There is a journey we all need to make, from anger, to peace, to forgiveness. Anger always destroys, peace always restores, and forgiveness always heals. This explains the journey, the steps you can take to make it happen for you.

1905047827 160pp **£7.99 $14.95**

IF You Fall...

It's a new beginning

Karen Darke

Karen Darke's story is about the indomitability of spirit, from one of life's cruel vagaries of fortune to what is insight and inspiration. She has overcome the limitations of paralysis and discovered a life of challenge and adventure that many of us only dream about. It is all about the mind, the spirit and the desire that some of us find, but which all of us possess.
Joe Simpson, mountaineer and author of *Touching the Void*

1905047886 240pp **£9.99 $19.95**

Love, Healing and Happiness

Spiritual wisdom for a post-secular era

Larry Culliford

This will become a classic book on spirituality. It is immensely practical and grounded. It mirrors the author's compassion and lays the foundation for a higher understanding of human suffering and hope. **Reinhard Kowalski** Consultant Clinical Psychologist

1905047916 304pp **£10.99 $19.95**

A Map to God
Awakening Spiritual Integrity
Susie Anthony

This describes an ancient hermetic pathway, representing a golden thread running through many traditions, which offers all we need to understand and do to actually become our best selves.
1846940443 260pp **£10.99 $21.95**

Punk Science
Inside the mind of God
Manjir Samanta-Laughton

Wow! Punk Science is an extraordinary journey from the microcosm of the atom to the macrocosm of the Universe and all stops in between. Manjir Samanta-Laughton's synthesis of cosmology and consciousness is sheer genius. It is elegant, simple and, as an added bonus, makes great reading. **Dr Bruce H. Lipton,** author of *The Biology of Belief*
1905047932 320pp **£12.95 $22.95**

Rosslyn Revealed
A secret library in stone
Alan Butler

Rosslyn Revealed gets to the bottom of the mystery of the chapel featured in the Da Vinci Code. The results of a lifetime of careful research and study demonstrate that truth really is stranger than fiction; a library of philosophical ideas and mystery rites, that were heresy in their time, have been disguised in the extraordinarily elaborate stone carvings.
1905047924 260pp b/w + colour illustrations **£19.95 $29.95** cl

The Way of Thomas
Nine Insights for Enlightened Living from the Secret Sayings of Jesus
John R. Mabry

What is the real story of early Christianity? Can we find a Jesus that is relevant as a spiritual guide for people today?

These and many other questions are addressed in this popular presentation of the teachings of this mystical Christian text. Includes a reader-friendly version of the gospel.

1846940303 196pp **£10.99 $19.95**

The Way Things Are
A Living Approach to Buddhism
Lama Ole Nydahl

An up-to-date and revised edition of a seminal work in the Diamond Way Buddhist tradition (three times the original length), that makes the timeless wisdom of Buddhism accessible to western audiences. Lama Ole has established more than 450 centres in 43 countries.

1846940427 240pp **£9.99 $19.95**

The 7 Ahas! of Highly Enlightened Souls
How to free yourself from ALL forms of stress
Mike George

7th printing

A very profound, self empowering book. Each page bursting with wisdom and insight. One you will need to read and reread over and over again!
Paradigm Shift.

I totally love this book, a wonderful nugget of inspiration.
PlanetStarz

1903816319 128pp 190/135mm **£5.99 $11.95**